LATIN ELEGIAC VERSE

LATIN ELEGIAC VERSE

A STUDY OF THE METRICAL USAGES OF TIBULLUS, PROPERTIUS & OVID

BY

MAURICE PLATNAUER

1971
Archon Books
Hamden, Connecticut

First published 1951

Reprinted 1971 with permission of
Cambridge University Press
in an unaltered and unabridged edition
as an Archon Book
The Shoe String Press, Inc.
Hamden, Connecticut 06514

ISBN 0-208-01116-1
Library of Congress catalog card number 79-143886

Printed in the United States of America

PREFACE

The object of this book is to provide, in a form as convenient as the material allows, a statement of the practice of the surviving Augustan elegists in their versification, their prosody, and certain points of word order and idiom. It draws attention to some of the metrical peculiarities of Roman elegy as compared with Greek, and also to the main technical differences between the Augustan elegiac poets. It should, I think, be useful to critics faced with metrical problems in expounding or editing an elegiac text and also to those not yet quite extinct *genera*, composers of Latin elegiac verse and their teachers in schools and colleges.

I should like to express my thanks to the University Press, and in particular to the readers and compositors for their skilful disposition of very refractory material, to Professor R. A. B. Mynors, whose careful scrutiny has saved me from many faults, to Mr Alan Ker for many valuable suggestions made while the book was still in a rudimentary form, and above all to Mr T. F. Higham, but for whose encouragement and help it would never have been completed.

M. P.

OXFORD
22 March 1951

CONTENTS

vii

CHAPTER I

Introduction

The poets whose works are considered in this book are:

(1) TIBULLUS

By 'Tibullus' is meant (*a*) the (genuinely Tibullan) poems of bks I and II, (*b*) bk III poems 1–6 inclusive, generally attributed to Lygdamus, (*c*) bk III poems 8–20, which will be referred to as the *Corpus Tibullianum*. If no distinction is drawn between these three sections of the extant poems the reference is 'Tib.', or 'Tibullus'. Where the authentic writings of the poet are differentiated from the rest the reference is 'Tib. I and II'; where the other two parts are differentiated the references are, respectively, 'Tib. (Lygd.)' and '*Corp. Tib.*'.

The number of lines (not couplets) in 'Tibullus' is: Tib. I and II, 1238; Tib. (Lygd.), 290; *Corp. Tib.*, 182; total, 1710.

(2) PROPERTIUS

The four books are referred to as Prop. I, II, III, and IV. The number of lines in these books is: bk I, 706; bk II, 1362; bk III, 988; bk IV, 952; total, 4008.

(3) OVID

Ovid's works are referred to by the following abbreviations:

Am. = Amores	*R.A.* = Remedia amoris
H. = Heroides	*Tr.* = Tristia
M.F. = Medicamina faciei	*P.* = Epistulae ex Ponto
A.A. = Ars amatoria	*F.* = Fasti

The *Ibis* is referred to without abbreviation.

PEV   I   I

Heroides I–XIV (the definitely genuine *Heroides*) are numbered in the usual way; the later (and possibly non-Ovidian) *Heroides* are numbered as follows:

XV.	Sappho–Phaoni
XVI.	Paris–Helenae
XVII.	Helene–Paridi
XVIII.	Leander–Heroni
XIX.	Hero–Leandro
XX.	Acontius–Cydippae
XXI.	Cydippe–Acontio

The number of lines in these works of Ovid is: *Am.*, 2456; *H.* I–XIV, 2192; *H.* XV–XXI, 1782; *M.F.*, 100; *A.A.* and *R.A.*, 3144; *Tr.*, 3532; *P.*, 3198; *Ibis*, 644; *F.*, 4972; total, 22,020.

Editions

Tibullus: Postgate² (Clarendon Press, Oxford, 1924)
Propertius: Phillimore² (Clarendon Press, Oxford, 1907)
Ov. *Am.*, *H.*, *M.F.*, *A.A.* and *R.A.*: Ehwald (Leipzig, 1903)
Ov. *Tr.*, *Ibis*, *P.*: Ehwald-Levy (Leipzig, 1922)
Ov. *F.*: Ehwald-Levy (Leipzig, 1924)

Phillimore's wayward text has often been deserted in favour of the saner readings of Butler and Barber's edition (Clarendon Press, 1933). The critical and exegetical editions of the *Heroides* by Palmer (Clarendon Press, 1898) and the *Tristia* by Owen (*P. Ovidi Nasonis Tristium libri V*, Clarendon Press, 1889, and *P. Ovidi Nasonis Tristium liber secundus*, Clarendon Press, 1924) have been much used.

Note: to ease reference Ehwald-Levy's attempt to split Ov. *Tr.* III. 4 and V. 2 each into two poems has been disregarded and the old (Merkel) numeration retained—as indeed it is by Ehwald-Levy in addition to the new.

Sigla

Abbreviations, such as those for the various caesuras and diaereses, have been explained in the chapters in which they occur. A vertical stroke (|) has been used throughout to mark the end of a foot or line; a dotted vertical stroke (⋮) to mark a caesura; both a vertical stroke and a dotted vertical stroke (⋮|) to indicate the coincidence of word- and foot-ending. The half-way point of the pentameter has been marked ‖. In the pentameter the four FULL feet are referred to as the first, second, third, and fourth foot respectively.

CHAPTER II

Versification

(a) CAESURA

Definition and notation

A caesura[1] is the division of a metrical foot between two
words. When the foot is a dactyl the split may be $-\mathbin{\vert}\cup\cup$
('strong' caesura), or $-\cup\mathbin{\vert}\cup$ ('weak' caesura), or $-\mathbin{\vert}\cup\mathbin{\vert}\cup$
('double' caesura). 'Double' caesuras are more apparent
than real, for nearly all short monosyllables are either enclitic
or proclitic. Thus:

> sunt $\vert$ in e|o (fuerant certe) delubra Dianae   Ov. *H.* xii. 69.

is strong;

> an sit $\vert$ ab | his omnis rigide submota libellis   Ov. *P.* iii. 3. 55.

is weak. Even where the monosyllables are neither enclitic
nor proclitic the sense, as shown by the punctuation, settles

---

[1] *Caesura* is a purely metrical term, though certain scholars, e.g. Cornu
(P. Lieger, *J. Cornus Beiträge zur lateinischen Metrik*, Vienna, 1927), have
tried to restrict it to cases in which there is a sense-pause, as well as a metrical
pause. It is true (so Sturtevant in *Am. J. Phil.* xlii, 1921, p. 304) that Ovid
shows a penchant for making a sense-pause at the main caesura of the hexameter (see p. 25), but that does not mean that where there is no sense-pause
there is no caesura. As P. B. Whitehead ('A new method of investigating the
caesura in the Latin hexameter and pentameter', *Am. J. Phil.* li, 1930, pp.
358–71), who opposes Cornu on this matter, points out, such a line as 'est
tamen *humani* $\vert$ *generis* iactura dolori' has a perfectly good caesura.

The constructive part of Whitehead's article, an attempt to prove that Ovid
consciously avoids certain inter-verbal consonantal collocations (he instances
-s n-, e.g. 'terrifico*s n*autas') except where there is a sense-pause, is not
convincing.

4

all doubts. Thus:

haec fac; ⋮ in | exiguo tempore liber eris   Ov. *Am.* II. 2. 40.

is weak, whereas

consulu|i ⋮ (nec en|im modice terrebar) anusque   Ov. *H.* V. 39.

is strong.

It follows that each of the first five feet of the hexameter has potentially a strong or a weak caesura; the sixth, being necessarily a spondee (or a trochee), can have only a strong caesura.

Notation used below will be: 1*s* (i.e. strong caesura in first foot), 1*w* (i.e. weak caesura in first foot), 2*s*, 2*w*, etc.

1. *The hexameter: caesuras considered foot by foot*

(i) 1*s*, 1*w*. No comment needed.

(ii) 2*s*. No comment.

2*w* is common, but used with this restriction—that it must be followed by a disyllabic word constituting an iambus, e.g.

cum tibi | maior ⋮ er|it fiducia, posse requiri   Ov. *A.A.* II. 349.

It cannot be followed by a trisyllable forming a bacchius (∪−−) (or by any longer word), because, as will be shown, there must be a caesura in the third foot. Theoretically, it might be followed by a trisyllable forming an amphibrach (∪−∪), but this was avoided because of the consequent 'lilt' (cf. the famous αὖτις ⋮ ἔ|πειτα ⋮ πέ|δονδε ⋮ κυ|λίνδετο | λᾶας ἀν|αιδής of *Od.* XI. 598, expressing by its sound the stone bumping downhill). Only five exceptions to the rule can be found:

quisquis am|ore ⋮ ten|etur, ⋮ e|at...   Tib. I. 2. 27.
non ego | totus ⋮ ab|esset ⋮ am|or...   Tib. I. 2. 63.

cum te | iussit ⁝ hab|ere ⁝ pu|ellam...   Prop. II. 33. 9.
aut in am|ore ⁝ dol|ere ⁝ vo|lo...   Prop. III. 8. 23.
et gravi|ora ⁝ re|pendit ⁝ in|iquis...   Prop. IV. 7. 41.

In the four apparent Ovidian examples:

et ven|dit quod utr|umque iuv|at...   *Am.* I. 10. 31.
siquis am|ans quod am|are iuv|at...   *R.A.* 13.
mollior | es nec ab|ire pot|es...   *R.A.* 529.
difficile | est quod, am|ice, mon|es...   *Tr.* V. 12. 3.

the first short of the second foot is proclitic, and the lines are really 2*s*, not 2*w*.

(iii) 3*s*, 3*w*.

The caesura in the third foot, owing to its regularity and central position, is commonly called '*the* caesura', a loose but useful expression.[1] In other feet a caesura is optional: here it may be regarded as obligatory. Its absence makes the hexameter (in common parlance) 'non-caesural'; but further distinctions and definitions are necessary. Thus:

(*a*) The term 'non-caesural' will be used of lines in which the third foot is entirely occupied by one word or part of a word, or by a preposition and the word it governs, e.g.

ferte et opes; ego | composit|o securus acervo   Tib. I. 1. 77.
tunc veniat licet | ad cass|es, inlaesus abibit *Corp. Tib.* III. 9. 17.

(*b*) Lines in which the first syllable of the third foot is a conjunction such as *et*, *sed*, or *nec* will be called 'quasi non-caesural', e.g.

at mihi per caed(em) | et facinus...   Tib. II. 4. 21.

---

[1] 'In Homer 98% of the lines, and in Ovid nearly 100% of the lines, contain a word-ending in the third foot. Because of the regularity with which it occurs...this word-ending is frequently designated as *the* caesura' (P. B. Whitehead, *loc. cit.* p. 358).

The rarity of non-caesural and quasi non-caesural lines in the three elegists is shown in the following table:

	(a) Non-caesural	(b) Quasi non-caesural	Percentage of (a)+(b)
Tibullus	12[1]	1[2]	Just under 2%
Propertius	45[3]	1[4]	Just over 2%
Ovid	9[5]	2[6]	0·1%

Quasi non-caesural lines must, *ex hypothesi*, have a diaeresis at the end of the second foot, and this diaeresis is found in all the non-caesural hexameters of Ovid and in most of those of Tibullus and Propertius. The only exceptions are:

Phoebe, sacras Messalinum...	Tib. II. 5. 17.
nullae sunt inimicitiae...	Prop. II. 8. 3.
pulverulentaque ad extremas...	Prop. III. 14. 7.
cum mihi somnus ab exsequiis...	Prop. IV. 7. 5.
Andromedeque et Hypermestre...	Prop. IV. 7. 63.
Cynthia gaudet in exuviis...	Prop. IV. 8. 63.

Absence of caesura in the third foot is usually compensated for by caesuras in both second and fourth feet, though sometimes in only one of these. The table on p. 8 gives the details.

---

[1] I. 1. 77; I. 5. 1; 27; I. 7. 61 (taking Baehrens's 'te canit agricola ⟨a⟩ magna...'); II. 3. 41; II. 5. 1; II. 6. 11; 49; III. 1. 9; III. 9. 17; III. 10. 13; III. 16. 5.

[2] II. 4. 21.

[3] I. 8. 25; 9. 1; 19. 25: II. 3. 1; 3; 5. 5; 6. 29; 37; 8. 3; 9. 9; 14. 3; 15. 19; 33; 51; 16. 7; 17. 11; 18. 19; 20. 13; 22. 41; 23. 3; 11; 24. 7; 23; 25. 39; 43; 28. 55; 29. 11; 30. 13; 33. 7; 34. 33: III. 3. 35; 6. 39; 9. 1; 11. 51; 14. 7; 21. 7; 17; 23. 21: IV. 3. 3; 5. 7; 7. 5; 63; 8. 35; 63; 83.

[4] I. 4. 13.

[5] *Am.* II. 10. 25; III. 1. 25; III. 9. 53; III. 15. 5; *H.* II. 37; XV. 113; *Tr.* IV. 10. 7; *F.* IV. 401; IV. 483.

[6] *F.* III. 585; VI. 443.

	Total non-caesural hexameters	2s+4s	2w+4s	4s only	2s only
Tibullus	12	9	–	3[1]	–
Propertius	45[2]	31	4[3]	8[4]	1[5]
Ovid	9	8	–	1[6]	–

The verse in Propertius, 'quem modo felicem invidia admirante ferebant' (II. 17. 11), is unique in having no caesura in second, third, or fourth foot.

Propertius in 37 examples out of 45 lightens the non-caesural hexameter by making the second foot a dactyl; Ovid does the same in seven out of nine;[7] Tibullus in nine only out of thirteen.

Conditions attaching to 3w are also of importance. As shown above, it is only five times preceded by 2w. Similarly, it may not be followed by 4w. In practice this means that mostly it is followed by a disyllable of iambic form.[8] For the only other possibilities are either (i) a trisyllable forming a bacchius, e.g.

quod tibi non utriusque petenti copia posta est   Cat. LXVIII. 39.

which seems to check the flow of the line by introducing what may be called a false ending, '—utriusque petenti ‖ ', and was

[1] I. 5. 1; I. 7. 61; III. 16. 5.
[2] It may be noted that there are no non-caesural lines in bk I.
[3] III. 14. 7; IV. 7. 5; IV. 8. 63; IV. 8. 83.
[4] II. 6. 29; II. 9. 9; II. 14. 3; II. 15. 33; II. 20. 13; II. 24. 7; II. 25. 39; III. 6. 39.
[5] IV. 8. 35.   [6] F. VI. 443.
[7] 'Siquid id est, usque a proavis vetus ordinis heres'; a line which occurs both at Am. III. 15. 5 and Tr. IV. 10. 7.
[8] W. Meyer (Zur Geschichte des griechischen und lateinischen Hexameters, Munich, 1883, p. 1050) calls 'the classic form' of the Ersatzcaesur (i.e. 3w) that in which it is preceded by 2s and followed by 4s. There are no cases in Tibullus or Ovid (except A.A. I. 293 cited below) in which 3w is not preceded by 2s, and in Propertius only seven: II. 29. 31; II. 32. 53; III. 2. 3; III. 8. 23; III. 11. 33; IV. 8. 61; IV. 10. 17.

consequently avoided;[1] or (ii) a quadrisyllable forming a second paeon ($\cup-\cup\cup$):

ut nostris tumefacta superbiat Umbria libris	Prop. IV. 1. 63.
Irus egens pecorisque Melanthius actor edendi	Ov. *H.* I. 95.
aspicit hos, ut forte pependerit aethere, mater	Ov. *F.* III. 863.

These three lines (and there are no others of the kind) do not offend the ear; and if the form is rare it is perhaps because such quadrisyllables are themselves uncommon; or (iii), uniquely, a word scanning $\cup---\cup$, viz.

illum Gnosiadesque Cydoneaeque iuvencae   Ov. *A.A.* I. 293.

Finally the ratio of $3s$ to $3w$ is a point of some interest, whether we compare Greek with Latin elegy, or the Latin elegists with one another. In the *Loutra Pallados* of Callimachus, 57% of the hexameters are $3w$, whereas the average for the Latin elegists is 8%. This is because Greek, as compared with Latin, has many more words ending in short open vowels and also many more that begin with a short vowel (e.g. the augment, compounds of ἐπι-, ἀπο-, etc.), to say nothing of the licence of shortening a final open long vowel before an initial short vowel.

The variation in the practice of the Latin elegists may be seen in the following table, which gives the percentages of $3w$:

Tib. I and II	20	Prop. II	4·4
Tib. (Lygd.)[2]	1·5	Prop. III	6·3
Corp. Tib.	18	Prop. IV	7·4
Prop. I	3·4		

[1] There is none in Tibullus; six in Propertius: II. 1. 51; 15. 43; 33. 9; 27; III. 6. 25: IV. 7. 41 (which also exhibits $2w$); and perhaps in Ovid (uniquely) 'alter amor tibi restat? habenda est altera Dido?' (*H.* VII. 17). This is Birt's emendation of a corrupt line (see Th. Birt, *Ad historiam hexametri latini symbola*, Bonn Diss., 1876, p. 14). Palmer prefers the late MSS. reading 'alter habendus amor tibi restat et . . .'.

[2] Only two cases: III. 4. 57 and III. 6. 17.

Ov. *Am.*	7·5	Ov. *A.A.* and *R.A.*	9
Ov. *H.* I–XIV	9	Ov. *F.*	8
Ov. *H.* XV–XXI	3·6	Ov. *Tr., P., Ibis*	4

Possibly Tibullus, the first of the three to adapt the Greek elegiac, consciously introduced as many weak caesuras as a refractory medium would allow, while his successors gave up the struggle and wrote a type of hexameter more consonant with the genius of the language.

(iv) 4*s*, 4*w*.

Here again Latin word-formation operates in favour of the strong caesura.[1] Percentages of 4*w* are:

Tib. I and II	1·5
Tib. I and II, Tib. (Lygd.), *Corp. Tib.*	2·7
Prop. I	1·4
Prop. IV	6
Prop. I, II, III, IV	4
Ov. *A.A.* and *R.A.*	4·4
Ov. *F.*	6·4
Ovid, the whole	6

The low percentage of Tib. I and II is to be expected, because his 3*w*, as we have seen, reach 20%, and 3*w* may not be followed (see above, p. 8) by 4*w*. Again, 4*w* is very rare when followed by 5*w*, e.g.

haec tibi fallaci resolutus ⦂ amore ⦂ Tibullus[2]   Tib. I. 9. 83.

---

[1] One argument against the attribution to Ovid of the *Consolatio* is the fact that over 10% of its hexameters show 4*w* (see p. 118).

[2] C. Cavallin, *De caesuris quarti et quinti trochaeorum hexametri apud latinos poetas coniunctis* (Lund, 1896). In the three books of Ov. *Am.* there are only five cases and in *A.A.* only six. Birt (*op. cit.* p. 28) notes five in *P.* II and III and one in *F.* IV.

(v) 5 s, 5 w.

Normally 5 s [1] must be preceded by a monosyllable [2] (thus producing 'bucolic diaeresis') and followed by a diaeresis after the fifth foot, e.g.

    quid tenera tibi coniuge opus? tua | si ⋮ bona | nescis

                                      Tib. I. 6. 33.

Tibullus violates the monosyllable 'rule' five [3] times, but in all these cases he has a diaeresis after the fifth foot, e.g.

    ...blandos of|fers ⋮ mihi | voltus   I. 6. I.

Propertius violates the monosyllable 'rule' five times. In three [4] of these examples he has a Greek word forming a minor ionic (∪∪−−) at the end, thus giving no diaeresis after the fifth foot. Not so in the two other examples:

    conteri|tur via | socco   II. 23. 15.
    poti|us precor | ut me   II. 24. 51.

Seven [5] out of the nine examples in Ovid end with a word forming a minor ionic or third paeon (∪∪−∪), the other two

  [1] Such lines as 'deque viro fias nec femina nec vir, ut Attis' (Ov. *Ibis* 455) are to be regarded as 5 w.
  [2] W. Meyer (*op. cit.* p. 1041) suggests that the Latin poets avoided 5 s, save where preceded by a monosyllable, to prevent, in lines which show (as many do) 2 s, 3 s, and 4 s, a superabundance of strong caesuras and the consequent continuous clash between word- and metrical accent, e.g. 'obliquó curréns spatió quantúm Capricornus' (Germ. *Aratea* 523). So, too, Vollmer (in Gercke-Norden's *Einleitung in die Altertumswissenschaft*, I, viii, p. 13).
  [3] I. 6. 1; 63; II. 4. 45; 59; II. 5. 111. At I. 2. 95 'circumterit' should be taken as one word.
  [4] 'refe|ras Ache|loi' (II. 34. 33); 'Orici|a tere|bintho' (III. 7. 49) (is this a conscious reminiscence of Virg. *Aen.* x. 136?); 'mer|ced(e) hya|cinthos' (IV. 7. 33).
  [5] 'in Maenali|a Ata|lanta' (*H.* IV. 99); 'cypressifer|o Ery|mantho' (*H.* IX. 87); 'Sithoni|o Aqui|lloni' (*H.* XI. 13); 'Nonacri|na Ata|lanta' (*A.A.* II. 185); 'Talaioni|ae Eri|phylae' (*A.A.* III. 13); 'purpure|as ame|thystos' (*ib.* 181); 'Naupacto|o Ache|loo' (*F.* II. 43).

(*F.* v. 83 and 87) with 'Atlante' and 'Cyllenes'. Apart from 'Aquiloni' the endings are all Greek words; and in seven out of the nine cases a quasi-Greek hiatus is observable.

Besides making a bucolic diaeresis in these hexameters which end in two disyllables the elegists almost always observed two further 'rules': (1) they made a sense-stop—anything from a (potential) comma to a full stop—at the bucolic diaeresis; (2) they made the fourth foot a dactyl. The norm, therefore, is such a line as:

> hoc vos praecipue, nive|ae, decet; | hoc ꞉ ubi | vidi
>
> Ov. *A.A.* III. 309.

In Tibullus, out of a total of sixteen lines ending in two disyllables, ten conform to this norm;[1] two[2] have a fourth-foot dactyl but no sense-pause, one[3] has a sense-stop but a fourth-foot spondee, and three[4] have neither sense-stop nor dactyl.

Propertius shows a total of thirteen,[5] twelve of which conform to the norm. The remaining case (II. 16. 25) has a sense-stop but a fourth-foot spondee.

Ovid has 31 cases, 27 of which conform to the norm. In one[6] there is no sense-pause, in one[7] a sense-pause but a fourth-foot spondee, and in two[8] neither sense-pause nor dactyl.

5 *w* needs no comment.

---

[1] Such a line as 'ure meum potius flamma caput et pete ferro' (I. 9. 21) is regarded as conforming to the rule, since a comma after 'caput' is optional. So, too, 'et seu longa virum terrae via seu vaga ducent' (II. 6. 3).

[2] I. 6. 33; II. 6. 7.

[3] III. 9. 15.

[4] I. 3. 5; II. 4. 51; III. 16. 1.

[5] Discounting '...sed fors et in hora' (II. 9. 1) where 'fors et' may be regarded as one word.

[6] *Am.* I. 4. 67.

Am. II. 17. 21.

[8] *H.* VII. 39; *Tr.* III. 10. 69.

(vi) 6s.

Many hexameters in the elegists apparently end with a monosyllable; but except in four[1] instances, another mono-syllable (or a disyllable) precedes in such a way that there is no caesura at all.[2] Monosyllabic substantives (*fas*, *mens*, *nil*, etc.) are followed by *est*; conjunctions (*et*, *aut*, *nec*, *si*, *ni*, *seu*, *an*, *cum*, *ut*, *quin*) and adverbs such as *non* and *nunc* are fol-lowed by monosyllabic parts of *esse*, or by relative, indefinite, or personal pronouns.

Ovid's 'apud quos' (*Tr.* II. 433; *P.* I. 3. 81) and 'ad os est' (*Tr.* v. 4. 5) are not exceptions, and Propertius's 'quid fles?' (II. 20. 1), if an exception, is an understandable one. The intractable examples are: 'amor qui' (Prop. II. 25. 17); 'quibus nos' (Ov. *P.* IV. 9. 101), and the more violent 'Aeonius fons' (*ib.* 2. 47; unique) and 'Cupido, est' (Ov. *Am.* II. 9. 47; apparently prodelision of *est* over a comma).

Hexameters rarely end with a five-syllable word: perhaps (besides Prop. I. 8. 35, 'Hippodamiae', and three proper nouns in Ovid) only Prop. II. 26. 15, 'increpitarent'. Quin-tilian calls such (and quadrisyllabic) endings 'permolle' (IX. 4. 65).

2. *The pentameter: caesuras considered foot by foot*

It will be convenient to consider first the main caesura, i.e. that which occurs at the half-way point in the line and which is followed by the third complete foot (here called the third foot). Its obligatory character was recognized by

[1] 'Minoia sella, et' (Prop. IV. 11. 21), accepted by Phillimore, is impossible. *Leg.* 'Minoida sellam' with Butler and Barber, *The Elegies of Propertius* (Oxford, 1933).

[2] See A. G. Harkness, 'The word-accent in Latin hexameters', *Class. Phil.* III (1908), p. 54, and O. Braum, *De monosyllabis ante caesuras hexametri latini collocatis* (Marburg Diss., 1906), pp. 72 sqq.

Quintilian, who writes of it, 'ut in pentametri medio spondeo, qui nisi alterius verbi fine, alterius initio constat, versum non efficit' (IX. 4. 98).

Points to observe are:

(*a*) that there are no exceptions to the use of this caesura apart from such cases as 'praeter ‖ vina' (Ov. *A.A.* I. 230), 'ultra ‖ limina' (*ib.* III. 418), and 'contra ‖ iusque piumque' (*H.* VIII. 4), in all of which places a disyllabic preposition[1] precedes, and the word it governs follows, the half-way point;[2]

(*b*) that elision at the caesura is not allowed. Catullus, it is true, has such lines as 'guttis abstersist(i) ‖ omnibus articulis' (XCIX. 8); but neither Tibullus nor Ovid used this licence, and Propertius did so twice only, viz. 'impun(e) ‖ illa' (I. 5. 32); 'Antaeiqu(e) ‖ Hesperidumque' (III. 22. 10). (For the apparent cases at Tib. I. 4. 56 and Prop. II. 14. 10 see p. 88.)

(i) 1 *s*, 1 *w* need no comment.

(ii) 2 *s* calls for no comment, nor does 2 *w* where the first foot is a spondee; but if 2 *w* is preceded by a dactyl we get a pentameter of which the two halves are metrically interchangeable. The extreme scarcity of such lines[3] suggests that

---

[1] That such were felt to be at least quasi-adverbial rather than strictly prepositional is clear from the fact that Ovid occasionally (e.g. *F.* I. 485–6; III. 23–4) ends a hexameter with *intra*, starting the pentameter with the word it 'governs'. So, too, Propertius, e.g. 'inter | proelia' (IV. 2. 3, 4).

[2] Where a genitive intervenes even a monosyllabic preposition can precede, and the governed substantive follow, the break; e.g. 'in muri ‖ membra' (Prop. III. 2. 6); 'cum Circi ‖ munere' (Ov. *F.* v. 190).

[3] W. Meyer (*op. cit.* p. 1033) comments on the rare occurrence of words of iambic form before the main caesura of the pentameter, both where the line starts with a spondee and where it starts with a dactyl. He notes only five instances in Tib. I and II, thirteen (out of a total of 386 pentameters) in Ov. *Am.* I, fourteen (out of a total of 395 pentameters) in Ov. *Am.* III, four

they were deliberately avoided. Percentages are: Tib. I and II, 0·7; Tib. (Lygd.), 1·4; *Corp. Tib.*, 3; Propertius, 3·7; Ovid, 2·5. When used, they often form a kind of jingle, e.g.

sive ea causa gravis, sive ea causa levis   Prop. II. 9. 36.
Nereidesque deae Nereidumque pater   Ov. *Am.* II. 11. 36.
semibovemque virum semivirumque bovem   Ov. *A.A.* II. 24.

In *Am.* I. 6 Ovid uses a 'reversible' pentameter as a refrain:

tempora noctis eunt; excute poste seram.

In Propertius and Ovid 17% of 'reversible' pentameters are jingles.

(iii) 3*s*, 3*w*. No comment, except as regards polysyllabic endings to the pentameter (see p. 17 below).

(iv) 4*s*.

This caesura means that the line ends with a word of three syllables forming either an anapaest or a tribrach[1]—an effect that was avoided. Taking strictly trisyllabic endings, i.e. regarding 'in foliis' (Prop. II. 20. 6), or 'et Calais' (Prop. I. 20. 26), or 'ut recitent' (Ov. *P.* III. 5. 40) as quadrisyllabic, we get the following results: Tibullus,[2] 20 = 3%; Propertius,[3] 30[4] = 1·5%; Ovid,[5] three only in 10,000 odd pentameters,

(out of 406) in Ov. *A.A.* III. That Ovid in his later work was less careful in this matter may be seen from the fact that in the first 200 pentameters of *F.* I there are 23 cases of an iambic word in this position.

[1] Apparent bi-caesural feet, e.g. 'non dat, habet' (Ov. *R.A.* 306); 'non sit amor' (Ov. *P.* I. I. 14) are of course 4*w*.

[2] Disregarding Tib. (Lygd.), who has three, and *Corp. Tib.*, which has two.

[3] R. Atkinson ('On the trisyllabic endings of the pentameter in Propertius', *Hermathena* I, 1874, pp. 276–85) endeavours to prove that 'no pentameter in Propertius ends in a trisyllable unless the word contains a liquid (usually in either the penultimate or the ultimate syllable)'. Even by classing the nasals as 'liquids' and 'emending' some lines that do not conform to his 'rule' he does not make his thesis convincing.

[4] 22 in bk I, eight in bk II, none in bks III or IV.

[5] *P.* I. I. 66; I. 8. 20; IV. 9. 26 are all more than doubtful readings.

and all of them in *P*., viz. 'scelus est' (I. 6. 27); 'liceat' (I. 8. 40); 'videor' (III. 6. 46).

Where a trisyllabic ending is found it is nearly always preceded by a word of iambic form,[1] e.g. 'vix excusari posse *mihi* videor' (Ov. *P*. III. 6. 46). This is so in seventeen out of the twenty in Tibullus; 24 out of the 30 in Propertius, and in all the Ovidian instances. For the most part these trisyllables are ordinary verbs and substantives; there are but few proper nouns ('Cilicas' and 'Venerem' at Tib. I. 7. 16; III. 6. 48; 'Venere', 'Zephyro', and 'Helena' at Prop. I. 14. 16; I. 16. 34; II. 34. 88).

A trisyllabic ending may have been avoided in order to prevent the rhythm's becoming anapaestic. E. H. Sturtevant (in *Trans. Am. Phil. Ass*. LV, 1924, p. 77), after pointing out that 'iambic words constitute only about 11·2% of a normal Latin vocabulary' and calling attention to the growing force of 'the iambic-ending rule' (only 37·9% of Catullus's pentameters end with an iambic word), concludes that the point of this ending was to help the harmony of metrical ictus and vocal stress in the earlier part of the second hemistich. Thus, if the pentameter ends 'ármaque saéva dédit' or 'ípsa iuvénca dábat', metrical ictus and vocal stress harmonize twice and clash only once; whereas in such an ending as 'delíciis lápidis' they clash twice and do not harmonize at all. There may be something in this, though it will not explain such endings as 'pax Ásiaeque fóret'.

[1] See A. Platt, *C.R.* XXXIV (1920), p. 168.

NOTE ON POLYSYLLABIC ENDINGS IN
THE PENTAMETER

These may be conveniently considered here in connexion with the preceding paragraph and with $3s$ and $3w$.

There is one instance of $3s$ followed by a six-syllable word: 'sis Berecynthiades' (Ov. *Ibis* 508). A disyllabic preposition followed by a five-syllable word which it governs, e.g. 'inter Hamadryadas' (Prop. II. 34. 76); 'inter ephemeridas' (*id.* III. 23. 20), must be regarded rather as forming a seven-syllable word than as an example of $3w$ followed by a quinquesyllable, as in 'magna pudicitiae' (Ov. *H.* XVI. 288).

Usage, as regards polysyllabic endings, is as follows:

	(a) 7 syllables	(b) 5 syllables	(c) 4 syllables
Tib. I and II[1]	–	5	18
Tib. (Lygd.)[1]	–	3	4
Corp. Tib.[1]	–	2	1
Propertius[2]	2	21	166
Ovid (excluding later *Heroides*)[3]	–	12	31

Of the Ovidian cases all but two of (b) and (c) occur in *Tr.* and *P.*, the two exceptions being quadrisyllables in *F.*, 'fluminibus' (v. 582); 'funeribus' (VI. 660). The later *Heroides* show 'pudicitiae' (XVI. 288); 'superciliis' (XVII. 16); 'deseruit' (XIX. 202).

Figures for Propertius's use of non-disyllabic endings as a whole are: bk I, 36%; II, $10\cdot5\%$; III, $2\cdot4\%$; IV, 1%. Butler and Barber (p. xvi) remark: 'Clearly the poet's maturer judgement preferred the sound of the disyllabic ending.'

[1] Five only of (b) and (c) in Tibullus are proper nouns.

[2] Four of (b) and 42 of (c) are proper nouns.

[3] Three of (b) and nine of (c) are proper nouns.

17

(b) DIAERESIS

Definition and notation

Diaeresis occurs where the end of a word is also the end of a foot. There are therefore five potential diaereses within a hexameter; and indeed a line attributed to Ennius displays all five and seems to justify the rule by which a caesura in the third foot became obligatory. The line is:

spársis | hástis | lóngis | cámpus | spléndet et | hórret

with its intolerable coincidence of metrical ictus and word stress.

Diaeresis after the first foot will be called 1*d*, after the second foot 2*d*, and so on.

1. *Diaeresis in the hexameter*

Only the following diaereses call for detailed comment: 2*d*, 3*d*, 4*d*. These will be taken in turn. Of 1*d* and 5*d* it may be said in passing that they seem to occur in about 50% of the hexameters of the elegists.

2*d*.

This diaeresis is rare (Tib. I and II, 9%; Tib. (Lygd.), 1%; *Corp. Tib.*, 14%; Propertius, 4·5%; Ovid, 2·5%) partly because it must be followed by either a monosyllable[1] or a trochee to make the caesura in the third foot; and partly because it would check the flow of the verse and produce a 'false ending' if the first two feet were constituted either by $-\cup\cup \;\vdots\!| --$, or by $-\cup \;\vdots\; \cup \;| --$, or by a word scanning $-\cup\cup--$ (cf. conditions attaching to 3*w*, i.e. weak caesura in third foot, p. 8 above).

---

[1] See O. Braum, *op. cit.* pp. 11 sqq.

Tibullus, whenever he has 2 *d*, makes a *strong* caesura in the second foot, e.g.

ludite: iam ⁝ nox | iungit equos...   II. 1. 87.

and does so even when the line does not begin $-\cup\cup--$, e.g.

urantur ⁝ pia | tura...   II. 2. 3.

Propertius in six examples has a *weak* caesura in the second foot, elision between second and third feet being present in all:

illi carus ⁝ eg(o) | et per me...	I. 8. 31.
regnave prima ⁝ Rem(i) | aut animos...	II. 1. 23.
tela fugacis ⁝ equ(i) | et bracati...	III. 4. 17.
sacra diesque ⁝ can(am) | et cognomina...	IV. 1. 69.
costum molle ⁝ dat(e) | et blandi...	IV. 6. 5.
dein quemcumque ⁝ loc(um) | externae...	IV. 8. 83.

In twenty[1] more he has no second foot caesura at all, but of all these twenty only six begin $-\cup\cup--$, and in these the 'false ending' is avoided by elision, e.g.

aut caner(em) | Aegypt(um) | et Nilum...[2]   II. 1. 31.

Ovid returns to the more careful usage of Tibullus. Out of his 260 odd 2 *d* lines only two are without a true strong caesura in the second foot, and both of these begin with two dactyls, so that there is no question of 'checked flow' or 'false ending':

haec anim(um) | – et quota | pars...	*H.* XII. 89.
praevolat | in medi(um), | et magna...	*F.* VI. 443.

[1] I. 21. 5: II. 1. 31; 3. 11; 14. 3; 15. 33; 17. 11; 20. 13; 24. 7; 24. 19; 25. 39; 28. 57: III. 3. 29; 6. 25; 6. 39; 9. 19; 12. 25; 16. 7; 21. 31; 22. 15: IV. 4. 31.
[2] The other five are: II. 17. 11; III. 3. 29; 9. 19; 12. 25; 21. 31.

19   2-2

3 d.

As caesura is necessary in the third foot, this diaeresis must be preceded either by a monosyllable or by a pyrrhic. Types of third and fourth foot, when 3 d is present, will therefore be:

	third foot	fourth foot	
(a)	$\cup$	$-\cup\cup$	e.g. ut expedit
(b)	$\cup$	$--$	e.g. dat illi
(c)	$-$	$-\cup\cup$	e.g. qua filia
(d)	$-$	$--$	e.g. spe noctis
(e)	$\cup\cup$	$-\cup\cup$	e.g. sua sidera
(f)	$\cup\cup$	$--$	e.g. tibi prosunt.

Of these (a), (c), (e), and (f), though not common, are normal; (b) is avoided in conjunction with 4 d (bucolic diaeresis) because of the 'checked flow' or 'false ending'. Types (d) and (f) are of particular interest because, when 4 d is also present, the two words can be transposed so as to avoid 3 d, unless sense or metre prevents. Thus 'noctis spe' could replace 'spe noctis' and 'prosunt tibi' could replace 'tibi prosunt'.

To take (f) first. In Tibullus at least twenty out of the 21 examples[1] avoid 3 d, i.e. the order 'prosunt tibi' is preferred. The same holds good for 44 out of the 46 examples in Propertius, and for 236 out of the 245 examples in Ovid. Moreover even in the exceptions we can generally see a reason for the 'tibi prosunt' form. In

aut quid *Erechthei tibi* prosunt carmina lecta?   Prop. II. 34. 29.

the poet is clearly echoing the word-order of

quid tua *Socraticis tibi* nunc sapientia libris

---

[1] The only instance in Postgate's edition (*O.C.T.*) is 'pauper erit praesto *tibi semper*; pauper adibit' (I. 5. 61). And here the text is disputable.

two lines above; and

> mollia Pegasides *date vestro* serta poetae   Prop. III. I. 19.

may be explained by a preference for putting imperatives and hortatory subjunctives first, at any rate when monosyllabic, e.g.

sit dives iure, furorem	Tib. I. I. 49.
fac ramum ramus adoptet	Ov. *R.A.* 195.
fac tecum multa loquatur	*ib.* 335.
sit vobis cura placendi	Ov. *M.F.* 23.

Ovid, in at least seven out of his nine examples (*Ibis* 85, 'male fido': *A.A.* II. 147; *Tr.* IV. 4. 15; *F.* I. 445, all 'quia – –': *A.A.* III. 403; *Tr.* II. 195; *ib.* 383, all 'nisi – –'), prefers keeping the natural word-order to avoiding 3 *d* by sacrificing it; not so in

> *cultis bene* Liber ab uvis   *A.A.* III. 101.

and

> *vectae male* virginis[1]   *Tr.* I. 10. 27.

But why did he write

> sed repetamus opus; *mihi nudis* rebus eundum est?
> *A.A.* III. 747.

We cannot say whether the motive of the elegists in their obvious preference for the order 'prosunt tibi' was the avoidance of 3 *d* or the lightening of the rhythm by means of a fourth-foot dactyl.

In their treatment of (*d*) above, 'spe noctis', the elegists show no such marked preference as in their treatment of (*f*)

---

[1] Note also, for wrenched word order to avoid 3 *d*, '*nostro sine* facta dolore' (Tib. III. 20. 3); 'talia. . .*propter mihi* verba' (Ov. *P.* IV. 14. 15).

except for Propertius, whose proportion of the 'noctis spe' to the 'spe noctis' type is three to one.[1]

Note in this general connexion that:

(*a*) monosyllabic parts of *esse* tend to follow spondaic words, e.g. 'rursus sum' (Ov. *Tr.* I. 3. 57), thus avoiding 3*d*;

(*b*) so too with monosyllabic personal pronouns, at least in Tibullus and Propertius. Ovid writes 'te dicam' and 'dicam te' indifferently;

(*c*) the postponed relative, e.g. 'frustra qui' instead of 'qui frustra', is on the whole preferred by both Propertius and Ovid, not by Tibullus;

(*d*) in all three elegists monosyllabic conjunctions (*si*, *sed*, *nec*, *vel*, *cum*, etc.) generally precede a fourth-foot spondee, thus producing 3*d*; but Ovid will sacrifice the natural order to secure chiasmus, e.g.

ille levi virga (*virgam nam...*)	*A.A.* II. 131.
dixit et a myrto (*myrto nam...*)	*A.A.* III. 53.

(*e*) in anaphora 3*d* is preferred by all three elegists, e.g.

me nova sollicitat, *me tangit* serior aetas   Ov. *Am.* II. 4. 45.

4*d*.

Bucolic diaeresis (4*d*), so important in Greek, was a matter of complete indifference to the Roman elegists. Its incidence happens to be a·little less in Ovid than in Tib. I and II and Propertius; but over the elegists as a whole the percentage only varies between 43 (Ov. *F.*) and 52 (Tib. I and II, and Prop. IV).

---

[1] Strictly speaking such a phrase as 'de rubro litore' is no more a case of 3*d* than 'rubro de litore'; but it is worthy of remark that the second type is far the commoner in all three elegists. Exceptions are 'de septem montibus' (Tib. II. 5. 55); 'de tincta murice' (Ov. *A.A.* I. 251); 'de magnis fontibus' (*R.A.* 97); 'sub nullo vindice' (*ib.* 145); 'de Bacchi munere' (*ib.* 803); 'post Tulli funera' (*F.* VI. 581).

2. *Diaeresis in the pentameter*

1 *d.*

When the first foot is a spondee followed by a strong mark of punctuation, this diaeresis occurs only twice in Tibullus (I. 4. 40; III. 13. 10); Propertius has:

servat(a). | an mediis	II. 14. 30.
liber: | tu	II. 21. 6.
dicat: | de nostro	II. 26. 24.
stamus: victrices	III. 22. 22.

and Ovid some eleven instances.[1]

1 *d* with the first foot a dactyl occurs about as often as not.

2 *d.*

Not counting the enclitic *est*, e.g. 'iustaque quamvis est ‖' (Ov. *P.* II. 8. 76), it may be said that normally where this diaeresis occurs it must be immediately preceded by a long monosyllable or else a word of pyrrhic form, e.g.

spes fovet et *fore* | cras semper ait melius	Tib. II. 6. 20.
infelix, *quod* | non alter et alter eras	Ov. *F.* v. 226.
at patriae *pater* | hic, ipsius ille fuit	Ov. *P.* I. 1. 36.

Such a line as Catullus's

o di, reddite | mi hoc pro pietate mea	LXXVI. 26.

would not have been written by his successors in elegy.

Many apparent examples of a pyrrhic preceding this diaeresis are not true examples at all, e.g. 'sine me', 'pudor est', etc. If the residue of true examples is small, this is rather because words of suitable form were scarce in Latin, than because 2 *d*, as such, was avoided; for Propertius does not scruple to write 'fruar \| o' (II. 1. 48); 'cinis \| heu' (II. 20. 16);

[1] *Am.* I. 6. 30; *H.* III. 24; IX. 24; IX. 150; XI. 128; XIV. 110; *A.A.* III. 764; *Tr.* III. 11. 6; *F.* III. 32; III. 758; V. 138.

'cinis | hic' (II. 11. 6); 'tibi | nunc' (II. 34. 58). Ovid's use is also unhesitating. It shows the following words coming immediately after the pyrrhic: *hic* (some part of), eleven times;[1] monosyllabic personal pronouns, six times;[2] *fit* twice;[3] *vir, dos, mens, vox*, and *par*, once each;[4] and once each, *dat, hinc* and *sic*.[5]

3 *d* occurs as often as not.

4 *d*.

Impossible, as the pentameter cannot end with a monosyllable. A. G. Harkness, in *Am. J. Phil.* XXXI (1910), p. 171, points out that monosyllabic pentameter endings are avoided as early as Catullus and as late as Ausonius. Martial has: 'amo | te' (I. 32. 2); 'et | hoc' (VII. 10. 12 and 14); 'dare | vis' (VII. 75. 2); and 'modo | das' (X. 16. 8). But 'sine te' (XII. 47. 2) should be regarded as a trisyllable. Besides these Harkness knows only of an inscription: 'et poteras ambos Italiae dare | tu' (Buecheler, *Carmina Latina Epigraphica*, 1187. 8).

(c) SENSE-PAUSES

Definition

By a sense-pause is meant the end of a sentence or clause marked by strong punctuation, i.e. a full stop, a colon, or a semicolon. Commas, parentheses shown by brackets or dashes, *oratio recta* introduced by *dixit*, e.g.

dixit: 'et hospitibus ianua nostra patet'   Ov. *F.* V. 502.

have not been regarded as indicating sense-pauses.

[1] *Am.* III. 2. 46; *H.* XVII. 52; *A.A.* I. 124; III. 552; *Tr.* I. 5. 40; II. 166; IV. 1. 38; *P.* I. 1. 36; IV. 10. 30; IV. 12. 8; *F.* IV. 34.
[2] *H.* XII. 86; XVII. 180; XIX. 206; *P.* I. 7. 54; III. 6. 12; *F.* I. 146.
[3] *Am.* I. 2. 10; *H.* XIX. 180.
[4] *A.A.* I. 524; III. 258; *P.* III. 3. 36; III. 5. 22; *Tr.* IV. 6. 26.
    Tr. III. 12. 52; IV. 3. 62; *F.* III. 206.

1. *In the hexameter*

The most frequent sense-pause in the elegiac couplet is that between the hexameter and the pentameter. Percentages are as follows:

Tib. I and II	10
Tib. (Lygd.) and *Corp. Tib.*	18
Prop. I	17·8
Prop. II–IV	24
Ov. *A.A.* and *R.A.*	31
Ov. *Am.* and *H.*	27·3
Ov. *F.*	22
Ov. *Tr.* and *P.*	13

Sense-pauses within the hexameter, as opposed to sense-pauses at the end, are comparatively rare. Ovid uses more than Tibullus and Propertius. Taking all the elegists together, percentages are roughly as follows:

at $3s$	5·6	at $1d$	0·4[1]
at $4s$	2	at $5w$	0·3
at $4d$	1	at $5d$	0·25
at $2s$	0·8	at $3w$	0·25[2]

$1w$. Pauses here are not found in Tibullus; in Propertius there is but one instance, 'deme: mihi certe…' (II. 18. 29); Ovid has six.[3]

$2w$. This is even rarer. Tib. I. 7. 5 has 'evenere: novos…'; Propertius none; Ovid perhaps only 'innuet illa: feras…' (*A.A.* II. 543).

[1] Many of these take the form of 'dixerat' followed by a full stop, e.g. 'dixerat. audibat iamdudum verba querentis' (Ov. *F.* III. 507). This is particularly common in the *Fasti*.

[2] 'vive pius: moriere; pius cole sacra: colentem' (Ov. *Am.* III. 9. 37), with pauses also at $2s$ and $5w$, is noteworthy.

[3] *H.* XII. 71; *Tr.* I. 3. 101; *P.* III. 2. 29; *ib.* 81; *F.* II. 265; VI. 89. In some other possible cases of this sense-pause (and of others) there is divergency of punctuation.

4 *w*. Of sense-pauses here perhaps only:

> cui dea 'ne nimium terrere! piabile fulmen'   Ov. *F.* III. 289.
> nox abiit, oriturque Aurora. parilia poscor   *ib.* IV. 721.

3 *d*. For this see, as the sole example:

> indicat auctorem locus? an, nisi nomine lecto Ov. *P.* I. 7. 3.

Sense-pauses seem never to occur at 1 *s*,[1] 2 *d*, 5 *s*, or 6 *s*.

2. *In the pentameter*

Here sense-pauses are altogether rarer than in the hexameter. The only ones used with any regularity by the three elegists are that at 1 *d*,[2] 2·7%; that at half-way point, 1·1%; that at 2 *s*, 1%. In the rarer sense-pauses there is a marked difference between the usage of Ovid and that of the two earlier elegists; thus:

1 *w*. In Tibullus only 'voce: palam...' (II. 1. 84); in Propertius only 'visere: at in lecto' (II. 29. 24) and 'possit: at ex omni...' (III. 21. 6). Yet Ovid has this pause some fifty odd times, half of these occurring in *F*.

3 *d*. Not in Tibullus; in Propertius only:

> cur haec tam dives? quis dedit? unde dedit?   II. 32. 42.

Ovid has at least a dozen instances.

3 *w*. Neither in Tibullus nor Propertius; Ovid has four, e.g.

> dextram tange: cruenta fuit   *Am.* III. 8. 16.

---

[1] Hexameters not infrequently start with 'quid?' (e.g. Prop. II. 8. 21; Ov. *Am.* I. 7. 7; Ov. *Tr.* II. 385, etc.), but this can scarcely be taken as a sense-pause.

[2] See p. 23.

4*w*. *Corp. Tib.* has

> quid miserum torques, rumor acerbe? tace!   III. 20. 4.

None in Propertius. Ovid has four, e.g.

> oscula ferre: tuli; proximus esse: fui   *Am.* III. 7. 48.

2*w*. Possibly the only case in the elegists is the last line quoted above, containing also a pause at 4*w*.

Sense-pauses never occur at 1*s*, 2*d*, 3*s*, 4*s*, or 4*d*.

(*d*) ENJAMBMENT OF COUPLETS

While the writers of Latin epic are concerned to avoid the coincidence, or at least the frequent coincidence, of sense- and line-ending, those of elegiac nearly always complete the sentence, or the clause, at the end of the pentameter. As in the section on sense-pauses, so here a full stop, a colon, or a semicolon at the end of the couplet will be regarded as forming a 'break'; a comma, or no mark of punctuation, will be treated as a case of enjambment.

A slightly increasing tendency away from enjambment is noticeable in the three elegists. The percentages of couplets ending with a comma or with no mark of punctuation are: Tibullus, 9%; Propertius, 7%; Ovid, 5%. All the elegists, Ovid not less than the others, indulge at times in long sentences or periods which may run on over four or five couplets. The following instances may be cited:

> tantum cara tibi quantum nec filia matri,
>   quantum nec cupido bella puella viro,
> pro qua sollicitas caelestia numina votis,
>   quae tibi securos non sinit ire dies
> et, cum te fusco Somnus velavit amictu,
>   vanum nocturnis fallit imaginibus,

carminibus celebrata tuis formosa Neaera
    alterius mavult esse puella viri,
diversasque suas agitat mens impia curas,
    nec gaudet casta nupta Neaera domo.

                                   Tib. (Lygd.) III. 4. 51–60.

quandocumque igitur vitam mea fata reposcent,
    et breve in exiguo marmore nomen ero,
Maecenas, nostrae spes invidiosa iuventae,
    et vitae et morti gloria iusta meae,
si te forte meo ducet via proxima busto,
    esseda caelatis siste Britanna iugis,
taliaque illacrimans mutae iace verba favillae—
    'huic misero fatum dura puella fuit'.

                                   Prop. II. 1. 71–8.[1]

per superos igitur, qui dant tibi longa dabuntque
    tempora, Romanum si modo nomen amant,
per patriam quae te tuta et secura parente est,
    cuius, ut in populo, pars ego nuper eram,
sic tibi, quem semper factis animoque mereris,
    reddatur gratae debitus urbis amor;
Livia sic tecum sociales compleat annos,
    quae, nisi te, nullo coniuge digna fuit,
quae si non esset, caelebs te vita deceret,
    nullaque, cui posses esse maritus, erat;
sospite sit tecum natus quoque sospes, et olim
    imperium regat hoc cum seniore senex;
ut faciantque tui, sidus iuvenale, nepotes,
    per tua perque tui facta parentis eant;
sic adsueta tuis semper Victoria castris
    nunc quoque se praestet notaque signa petat,
Ausoniumque ducem solitis circumvolet alis,
    ponat et in nitida laurea serta coma,
per quem bella geris, cuius nunc corpore pugnas,
    auspicium cui das grande deosque tuos,

                _____

    [1] See also I. 11. 1–5; III. 11. 39–46.

dimidioque tui es praesens et respicis urbem,
    dimidio procul es saevaque bella geris;
hic tibi sic redeat superato victor ab hoste,
    inque coronatis fulgeat altus equis—
parce, precor, fulmenque tuum, fera tela, reconde,
    heu nimium misero cognita tela mihi.

Ov. Tr. II. 155–80.[1]

Such periods as these, however, are rare, and it is not often that more than two couplets are found together without the occurrence of some major punctuation mark. The two couplets so joined together may either be:

(1) paratactic, the one to the other; or

(2) subordinate, the first to the second or the second to the first.

(1) The commonest form of parataxis, that effected by means of the conjunctions *et, sed, aut, nec, -que, -ve,* etc., is too common to need illustration. Another form, particularly frequent in Tibullus, is anaphora, e.g.

                    . . . Tarbella Pyrene
        testis et Oceani litora Santonici,
        testis Arar . . .   Tib. I. 7. 9–11.

        multis ista dabunt *litora* discidium,
        litora quae fuerant castis inimica puellis

Prop. I. 11. 28–9.

        ut cum populeas ventilat aura comas,
        ut leni Zephyro gracilis vibratur harundo

Ov. Am. I. 7. 54–5.

(2) Subordinate clauses of all types are to be found, either preceding the main sentence, and thus forming the first of two or more couplets, or following it, and thus forming the second or last; they occur so often that it is unnecessary to

[1] See also *H.* VII. 157–63.

give instances.[1] A rarer form is that in which there is found
in the hexameter or pentameter of one couplet an adjective
or participle in agreement with a substantive in the other, e.g.

> ut Messalinum celebrem, cum praemia belli
>   ante suos currus oppida victa feret,
> ipse gerens laurus   Tib. II. 5. 115–17.

> (Achilles) viderat informem multa Patroclon harena
>   porrectum et sparsas caede iacere comas,
> omnia formosam propter Briseida passus   Prop. II. 8. 33–5.

> ecce, mero dubii, comitum clamore frequentes,
>   flore novo madidas impediente comas,
> in thalamos laeti...feruntur[2]   Ov. H. XIV. 29–31.

In two types of case the main sentence, or a clause, is not
completed within the framework of the first couplet and is
thus obliged to run over into the next:

(*a*) When a parenthesis occurs (generally in the first pentameter), e.g.

> et mihi praecipue, iaceo cum saucius annum
>   et (faveo morbo cum iuvat ipse dolor)
> usque cano Nemesim...   Tib. II. 5. 109–11.

> quarum nulla tua fuerit mihi, Cynthia, forma
>   gratior, et (Tellus hoc ita iusta sinat)
> quamvis...,
>   cara tamen lacrimis ossa futura meis   Prop. I. 19. 15–18.

> sed (tua sic domitis Parthae telluris alumnis
>   pura triumphantis hasta sequatur equos)
> incorrupta mei conserva foedera lecti   Prop. IV. 3. 67–9.

---

[1] A rather extreme case in Propertius may be noticed:

> 'gavisa est certe sublatam Cynthia legem,
>   qua quondam edicta flemus uterque diu,
>   ni nos divideret'   II. 7. 1–3.

[2] See also H. XIII. 58–9.

cum Phoebus...
  (nam tulit iratos mobilis una Notos)
astitit Augusti puppim super   Prop. IV. 6. 27–9.

qua penetrat (virgo, tale iter omne cave)
  ieiuni serpentis honos   Prop. IV. 8. 6–7.

institeram quare primi Megalensia ludi
  urbe forent nostra, cum dea (sensit enim)
'illa deos' inquit 'peperit'   Ov. *F.* IV. 357–9.

(*b*) With vocatives. This is particularly common in Ovid, who often, by qualifying a vocative with relative clauses or participles, extends his sentence over several couplets. Propertius[1] offers a number of simple instances, e.g.

Maecenas, eques Etrusco de sanguine regum,
  intra fortunam qui cupis esse tuam,
quid me...mittis...?   III. 9. 1–3.

But the Ovidian[2] cases are more complicated, e.g.

colligere incertos et in ordine ponere crines
  docta nec ancillas inter habenda Nape,
inque ministeriis furtivae cognita noctis
  utilis et dandis ingeniosa notis,
saepe venire ad me dubitantem hortata Corinnam,
  saepe laboranti fida reperta mihi,
accipe...tabellas   *Am.* I. 11. 1–7.

o mihi dilectos inter pars prima sodales,
  unica fortunis ara reperta meis
cuius ab adloquiis anima haec moribunda revixit,
  ut vigil infusa Pallade flamma solet;
qui veritus non es portus aperire fideles
  fulmine percussae confugiumque rati;

------

[1] See also IV. 4. 31–3; IV. 6. 37–9.
[2] See also *Am.* II. 8. 1–5; *Tr.* IV. 3. 1–10.

cuius eram censu non me sensurus egentem,
    si Caesar patrias eripuisset opes;
temporis oblitum dum me rapit impetus huius,
    excidit, heu, nomen quam mihi paene tuum

Tr. IV. 5. 1–10.

This 'run on' with the vocative is particularly characteristic
of Ovid, when an adjurative *per* is used, expressing the
speaker's hopes for the addressee, with a *sic* clause (or several
sic clauses) or without, should the latter grant his request.
Instances[1] are:

Isi, Paraetonium genialiaque arva Canopi
    quae colis et Memphin palmiferamque Pharon,
quaeque celer Nilus lato dilapsus in alveo
    per septem portus in maris exit aquas,
per tua sistra precor, per Anubidis ora verendi,
    sic tua sacra pius semper Osiris amet,
pigraque labatur circa donaria serpens,
    et comes in pompa corniger Apis eat:
huc adhibe vultus, et in una parce duobus   *Am.* II. 13. 7–15.

at tu per studii communia foedera sacri,
    per non vile tibi nomen amicitiae,
sic capto Latiis Germanicus hoste catenis
    materiam vestris adferat ingeniis;
sic valeant pueri, votum commune deorum,
    quos laus formandos est tibi magna datos,
quanta potes, praebe nostrae momenta saluti,
    quae nisi mutato nulla futura loco est   *P.* IV. 13. 43–50.

Outside the types mentioned above true enjambment is very
rare. From Propertius may be cited:

atque ubi iam nostris lassavit bracchia plagis,
    Lygdamus ad plutei fulcra sinistra latens
eruitur   IV. 8. 67–9.

---

[1] See also *Tr.* V. 2. 47–54; V. 3. 35–44.

Claudius a Rheno traiectos arcuit hostis,
  Belgica cum vasti parma relata ducis
Virdomari   IV. 10. 39–41.

From Ovid:

  mane erat, et thalamos cara recepta soror
  disiectamque comas adversaque in ora iacentem
    invenit   *H*. XII. 62–4.

  languor et immodici sub nullo vindice somni
    aleaque et multo tempora quassa mero
  eripiunt omnes...... ....nervos   *R.A.* 145–7.

(*e*) EPANALEPSIS

Epanalepsis, or the repetition of a word or phrase after intervening matter, is often found in the elegists, either

(1) within the couplet, when a word in the hexameter is repeated appositionally in the pentameter; or

(2) between couplets, where a word in the first pentameter is so repeated in the hexameter of the second couplet.

1. The repeated word is found as a rule (*a*) ultimate, (*b*) penultimate, or (*c*) antepenultimate in the hexameter and again as first word in the following pentameter, e.g.

(*a*) vos tenet...... ....*unda*,
      unda...non adeunda...   Tib. (Lygd.) III. 5. 1–2.
      haec...ludebat...*Varro*, | *Varro*...   Prop. II. 34. 85–6.
      consurgit vertice *murus*, | *murus*...   Prop. IV. 1. 125–6.

(*b*) largibar *munera* somno, | *munera*...   Prop. I. 3. 25–6.
      percurrens *luna* fenestras, | *luna*...   Prop. I. 3. 31–2.
      pocula Phaedrae, | *pocula*...   Prop. II. 1. 51–2.
      caneret tibi *tibia* somnos, | *tibia*...   Prop. II. 7. 11–12.
      meruit mea *gloria* nomen, | *gloria*...   Prop. II. 7. 17–18.
      Umbria libris, | *Umbria*...   Prop. IV. 1. 63–4.
      devota est *ara* repertis, | *ara*...   Prop. IV. 9. 67–8.

pia *vota* puellae, | *vota*. . .   Ov. *Am.* II. 6. 43–4.
fila dedissem, | *fila*. . .   Ov. *H.* X. 103–4.
oscula iungis, | *oscula*. . .   Ov. *H.* XVIII. 101–2.
urbe Quirini, | *urbe*. . .   Ov. *Tr.* I. 8. 37–8.
stamina nostri, | *stamina*. . .   Ov. *Tr.* IV. 1. 63–4.

(*c*) te *somnia* nostra reducunt, | *somnia*. . . Ov. *H.* XV. 123–4.

The first occurrence of the word seldom goes back further than the antepenultimate; but we find

> *lumina*que in gremio veluti defixa tenebam,
> *lumina*. . .   Ov. *H.* XXI. 113–14.

Occasionally also the word, when repeated in the pentameter, occupies other than the first place,[1] e.g.

> per tamen *ossa* viri. . .
> semper iudiciis *ossa* verenda meis   Ov. *H.* III. 103–4.

Ovid is fond, too, of repeating at the end of the pentameter a phrase which he has used to begin the hexameter, e.g.

> *Ilia, pone metus.* tibi regia nostra patebit,
> teque colunt omnes. *Ilia, pone metus*   *Am.* III. 6. 61–2.

Other instances of this may be found at *H.* V. 117–18; XV. 213–14; *R.A.* 385–6; *F.* II. 235–6; IV. 365–6.[2]

2. Normally the repeated words are (*a*) at the end of the pentameter and the beginning of the hexameter, e.g.

> tibi *rapta dabit*. | *rapta dabit* primo. . .   Tib. I. 4. 54–5.[3]
> *eheu*, tu mihi *certus eras*,
> *certus eras, eheu*. . .   Prop. II. 24. 36–7.

---

[1] If 'fata' in Prop. II. 28. 26 is correct, we get a Propertian example; but almost certainly 'facta' should be read (so Butler and Barber).

[2] In the early Middle Ages elegiacs of which the end half of the pentameter repeated the first 2½ feet of the hexameter became a recognized genre. They were called 'echoing', 'serpentine', or 'reciprocal' elegiacs (see *Baedae Opera Historica*, ed. Plummer, vol. II, p. 241). For a later 'classical' example, see Martial IX. 97, where every hexameter begins, and every pentameter ends, with 'rumpitur invidia'.

[3] If this be, as it almost certainly is, the correct reading.

ipsa perit. | *ipsa perit . . .*	Ov. *Am.* II. 14. 38–9.
arma dabit; | *arma dabit . . .*	Ov. *H.* XIII. 140–1.
Daulias *ales Ityn:* | *ales Ityn . . .*	Ov. *H.* XV. 154–5.
ille secundus erat; | *ille secundus erat . . .*	Ov. *H.* XXI. 72–3.
'quid mihi fiet?' ait.	
'quid mihi fiet?' ait . . .	Ov. *A.A.* I. 536–7.
rude *tempus erat.* | *tempus erat . . .*	Ov. *Tr.* IV. 8. 24–5.
me quoque *posse puta.* | *posse puta . . .*	Ov. *Tr.* V. 8. 34–5.
ferret opem: | *ferret opem* certe . . .	Ov. *F.* II. 400–1.
non est *carminis huius opus.*	
carminis huius opus causas exprimere . . .	Ov. *F.* III. 724–5.
gravidae posceris *exta bovis.*	
exta bovis gravidae dantur . . .	Ov. *F.* IV. 670–1.
si *favet alma Pales.* | *alma Pales, faveas . . .* Ov. *F.* IV. 722–3.	

Sometimes (*b*) a word or words occurring *before* the end of the pentameter are repeated at the beginning of the following hexameter, e.g.

vincula portet Amor, | *vincula . . .*	Tib. II. 2. 18–19.
fistula sacra deo, | *fistula . . .*	Tib. II. 5. 30–1.
increpat usque moras.	
increpat usque licet . . .	Ov. *H.* I. 82–3.
quis credat pueris *non nocuisse* feram?	
non nocuisse parum est . . .	Ov. *F.* II. 414–15.

And occasionally (*c*) the final words of the pentameter are repeated *later* than at the beginning of the hexameter, e.g.

facilis . . . *mens* sit et *apta capi.*	
mens erit *apta capi . . .*	Ov. *A.A.* I. 358–9.

Very rarely epanalepsis leaps a whole line, the repeated word occurring in each hexameter of two contiguous couplets, e.g.

tunica tua *pectora* laxa,	
atque oculis aditum nuda dedere meis,	
pectora . . .	Ov. *H.* XVI. 249–51.

CHAPTER III

Analysis of the Elegiac Couplet

(a) DACTYLS AND SPONDEES[1]

In the first four feet of the hexameter and the first two of the pentameter the elegiac poets were free to use what combination of dactyls and spondees they pleased.

In the hexameter the alternatives number sixteen and are (D = dactyl; S = spondee):

1. *DDDD*	2. *DDDS*	3. *DDSD*	4. *DDSS*
5. *DSDD*	6. *DSDS*	7. *DSSD*	8. *DSSS*
9. *SDDD*	10. *SDDS*	11. *SDSD*	12. *SDSS*
13. *SSDD*	14. *SSDS*	15. *SSSD*	16. *SSSS*

In the pentameter four:

1. *DD*	2. *DS*	3. *SD*	4. *SS*

An examination of Ov. *A.A.* II together with a similar number of lines (746) from Tib. I and Prop. II yields the following results:

HEXAMETER:

Type	Tibullus Number	Tibullus Percentage	Propertius Number	Propertius Percentage	Ovid Number	Ovid Percentage
1. *DDDD*	7	1·8	5	1·3	25	6·7
2. *DDDS*	35	9·2	17	4·7	34	9
3. *DDSD*	21	5·8	24	6·6	38	10
4. *DDSS*	53	14·2	32	8·6	45	12
5. *DSDD*	16	4·2	9	2·4	36	9·5

[1] This subject has been exhaustively studied by E. F. Hultgren in an article entitled 'Statistische Untersuchungen des Distichons', *Berichte der sächs. Ges. der Wiss.* (Leipzig, 1872), pp. 1–28.

ANALYSIS OF THE ELEGIAC COUPLET

Type	Tibullus Number	Tibullus Percentage	Propertius Number	Propertius Percentage	Ovid Number	Ovid Percentage
6. *DSDS*	53	14·1	43	11	51	13·8
7. *DSSD*	24	6·6	22	6	40	10·7
8. *DSSS*	74	20	61	16·5	50	13·7
9. *SDDD*	3	0·8	10	2·8	6	1·6
10. *SDDS*	17	4·7	11	3	11	3
11. *SDSD*	8	2·1	19	5	9	2·4
12. *SDSS*	19	5	44	12	8	2·1
13. *SSDD*	2	0·5	5	1·3	6	1·6
14. *SSDS*	16	·4·2	28	7·5	8	2·1
15. *SSSD*	8	2·1	11	3	2	0·5
16. *SSSS*	17	4·7	32	8·6	4	1

PENTAMETER:

Type	Tibullus Number	Tibullus Percentage	Propertius Number	Propertius Percentage	Ovid Number	Ovid Percentage
1. *DD*	89	24	90	24·1	115	30·9
2. *DS*	218	58·6	161	43	195	52·4
3. *SD*	20	5·2	62	16·5	31	8·3
4. *SS*	46	12·2	60	16·4	32	8·4

It can be seen from these figures (1) that in all three poets the lines beginning with a dactyl (types 1–8 in the hexameter, 1–2 in the pentameter) greatly outnumber those beginning with a spondee (types 9–16, 3–4); (2) that this preference for a dactylic opening, marked even in Propertius, is stronger in Tibullus and stronger still in Ovid.[1]

In all the works of the three elegists the lines (hexameter and pentameter) which begin with a spondee are, in number and percentage, as shown on p. 38.

[1] R. S. Radford (*Trans. Am. Phil. Ass.* LI, 1920, p. 149) observes that, as the Greek language is twice as rich in dactyls as in spondees, while in Latin this relation is reversed, Tibullus and, still more, Ovid were consciously striving against the natural (spondaic) character of the language, whereas Propertius, following Catullus (who shows only 37% dactyls to Ovid's 57%), allowed himself to take the line of least resistance and so wrote more 'spondaically'.

	Number of couplets	Hexameters starting with spondee	Percentage	Pentameters starting with spondee	Percentage
Tib. I and II	619	142	23	104	17
Tib. (Lygd.)	145	64	44·5	58	40
Corp. Tib.	91	26	29	36	40
Prop. I	353	144	41	71	20
Prop. II	681	293	43	218	32
Prop. III	494	179	36·5	155	31
Prop. IV	476	129	27	128	27
Ov. Am.	1228	246	20	275	22·4
Ov. A.A., R.A., M.F.	1622	293	18	303	18·7
Ov. H. I–XIV	1096	188	17	210	20
Ov. H. XV–XXI	891	132	15	201	22·5
Ov. F.	2486	265	10·7	503	20
Ov. Tr., P., Ibis	3687	525	14·2	889	24

Nothing very striking emerges from these figures, except perhaps the comparative 'lightness' of the Ovidian openings already mentioned, a lightness which seems to increase in his later works.[1] It seems also that Ovid is a little more prone to initial dactyls in hexameters than in pentameters.

(b) SPONDAIC HEXAMETERS

The rule which in the Latin hexameter demanded a dactyl in the fifth foot is seldom broken by the elegists. The tendency noticed by Cicero[2] in the younger Graecizing poets of his day towards the use of spondaic hexameters (i.e. hexameters in which the fifth foot is a spondee) was presumably restricted

---

[1] R. S. Radford's attempt (loc. cit.) to show that Ovid during the course of his life wrote, in general, more and more 'dactylically' is not very convincing, depending, as it largely does, on the arbitrary assumption that the more spondaic poems in the Amores come from the first edition of that work.

[2] Ad Att. VII. 2. 1: 'ita belle nobis "flavit ab Epiro lenissimus Onchesmites". hunc σπονδειάζοντα, si cui voles τῶν νεωτέρων, pro tuo vendito.'

to the writers of hexameter verse.[1] Such endings, effective and beautiful as they are, are at any rate seldom used by the poets under consideration, and when used almost always take the form of Greek words. These words are generally quadrisyllabic, and, when trisyllabic, are more often than not found in conjunction with a 'Greek' hiatus.[2]

In Tibullus, no instance.

In Propertius, quadrisyllables (Greek): 'heroinis' (I. 13. 31), 'heroinae' (I. 19. 13), 'heroine' (II. 2. 9), 'Orithyiae' (I. 20. 31 and III. 7. 13), 'Thermodonta' (IV. 4. 71); quadrisyllables (Latin): 'formosarum' (II. 28. 49).

In Ovid, quadrisyllables (Greek): 'Orithyiae' (*Am.* I. 6. 53), 'Ilithyia' (*Am.* II. 13. 21), 'Aeetine' (*H.* VI. 103), 'Cyllenea' (*A.A.* III. 147), 'Nonacrini' (*F.* II. 275), 'Atlanteas' (*F.* III. 105), 'Hellespontum' (*F.* IV. 567), 'Hippocrenes' (*F.* V. 7), 'Uriona' (*ib.* 535), 'Amphitrite' (*ib.* 731), 'Hellesponti' (*F.* VI. 341); quadrisyllables (Latin): 'elisissent' (*H.* XII. 121, preceded by the Greek word 'Symplegades'), 'Collatini' (*F.* II. 787); trisyllables (Greek): 'Amyclaeo Polluci' (*H.* VIII. 71—certainly spurious), 'Aeonii Alcidae' (*H.* IX. 133), 'lotifero Eueno'[3] (*ib.* 141), 'caelifero Atlante' (*F.* V. 83), 'cupressiferae Cyllenes' (*ib.* 87).

---

[1] Callimachus himself, though he has many spondaic lines in his hexameter poems, avoided them in elegiacs; and Catullus followed his practice, ending (in his elegiac poems) only two hexameters with spondees (c. 1, the intractable proper noun 'Aufilenam', and CXVI. 3, 'conarere'). See E. Norden, *P. Vergilius Maro, Aeneis Buch VI*[3] (Teubner, 1926), p. 438.

[2] See p. 11.

[3] If Bentley's and Heinsius's emendations be accepted.

(c) THE FINAL WORD OF THE LINE

1. *In the hexameter*

The elegiac poets seem to have avoided epithets at the end of the hexameter. Over 80% of their hexameters end in substantives or verbs, and adjectives do not total much more than 2%. One type of hexameter ending all three avoided almost entirely, that is, substantives ending in -*ă* (feminine singular or neuter plural) followed by a qualifying adjective. Tibullus has 'omina dira' (I. 3. 17), 'glarea dura' (I. 7. 59); Propertius has 'tela caduca' (IV. 2. 53); and Ovid has 'adultera cara' (*Am.* III. 4. 29). Ovid occasionally ends a hexameter with a preposition governing the first word of the pentameter, e.g. '...proque | Caesare...' (*Tr.* I. 2. 103–4); '...intra | fortunam...' (*Tr.* III. 4. 25–6); '...inter | quos...' (*Tr.* V. 7. 9–10); '...infra | te...' (*ib.* 8. 1–2). See p. 99.

2. *In the pentameter*

About 80% of all the pentameters of the three elegists (who do not differ among themselves on this point) end with a substantive or a verb.[1] About 17% end with a pronoun. Of these pronouns the possessives are the commonest, but the metrically possible forms of the personal pronouns, *ego, mihi, tibi, sibi,* are also frequently found. Rarer pronouns are the interrogative *uter* (Ov. *A.A.* I. 168; *F.* IV. 812), the demonstratives[2] *eum* (only Prop. II. 29. 8), *eam* (only Ov. *F.* VI. 434),[3] and *idem.*[4] The remaining (roughly) 3% is composed of adverbs, conjunctions, numerals, and adjectives.

In this 80% is included prodelided *est* (or *es,* e.g. 'dea es', Prop. II. 33. 14), which can follow any open final vowel, long or short (-*u* rarely; perhaps only 'manu est', Ov. *P.* IV. 1. 14), or diphthong, or -*m.* 'Sat est' is also found (e.g. Prop. I. 2. 26; II. 6. 40; II. 10. 6; IV. 1. 146; IV. 9. 36).

[2] Also 'ea est' (Ov. *F.* V. 150). See pp. 116–17.

[3] This very uncertain reading is accepted by Frazer.

[4] E.g. Ov. *A.A.* II. 128; *R.A.* 628; *Tr.* II. 58; III. 4. 78.

ADVERBS. The following are found:

diu (Prop. I. 10. 22; II. 5. 8; II. 7. 2; II. 25. 34: Ov. *H.* VII. 182; XI. 120; *A.A.* II. 692; *R.A.* 416; *P.* I. 6. 12; I. 10. 14; II. 8. 42; *F.* II. 844).

heri (Prop. II. 14. 20; III. 23. 12: Ov. *F.* II. 76).

ita (Ov. *F.* III. 436).

magis (*Corp. Tib.* III. 13. 2: Prop. I. 1. 22; II. 9. 38; III. 19. 2: Ov. *P.* III. 3. 72; III. 5. 12).

minus (Prop. II. 32. 46: Ov. *P.* II. 2. 44; III. 1. 98; IV. 12. 22; IV. 15. 42).

palam (*Corp. Tib.* III. 11. 18: Ov. *Am.* III. 14. 8; *Tr.* III. 14. 18; IV. 5. 12).

parum (Prop. III. 7. 34 (parum est): Ov. *Am.* I. 6. 22; *H.* XIV. 82; *Tr.* III. 8. 18; III. 11. 38; IV. 2. 26; *P.* III. 7. 12).

prius (Ov. *P.* IV. 1. 16; *F.* I. 632; VI. 750).

procul (Ov. *Am.* III. 5. 28; *F.* IV. 116).

quater (Ov. *F.* III. 880).

satis (Ov. *F.* I. 34).

semel (Tib. I. 9. 6; II. 6. 42: Prop. II. 30. 10: Ov. *R.A.* 294; *Tr.* II. 26; II. 210; *F.* III. 480).

simul (Prop. II. 6. 12: Ov. *P.* IV. 6. 16; *F.* I. 140).

super (Ov. *F.* II. 748; V. 600).

tamen (Tib. (Lygd.) III. 1. 6; III. 6. 56: Prop. I. 15. 32; II. 8. 28: Ov. *A.A.* I. 228, 478, 664, 700; *Tr.* I. 5. 82; *P.* IV. 8. 2; *F.* II. 688).

CONJUNCTIONS. *enim* is found at Ov. *F.* IV. 358, in the parenthesis '(sensit enim)'.

NUMERALS. All the metrically possible forms are found except *tria*: *duo* (-*os*, -*as*) constantly (e.g. Ov. *A.A.* I. 684); *trium* (e.g. Ov. *F.* III. 802); *tribus* (e.g. Prop. IV. 10. 2); *novem* (e.g. Ov. *A.A.* I. 648); *decem* (e.g. Ov. *A.A.* I. 436).

ADJECTIVES. These may be classified under seven headings, though the usages often shade off from one category into another.

(1) *Adjectives used predicatively*

As a predicative adjective is virtually a verb (e.g. *esse ruber = rubere*) such are freely used as last word of the pentameter, e.g.

est mihi supplicii causa fuisse *piam*	Ov. *H*. XIV. 4.

Less simple cases of adjectives used predicatively are:

nempe tulit fastus ausa rogare *prior*[1]	Prop. IV. 5. 42.
ante fores dominae condar oportet *iners*	Prop. III. 7. 72.
sic nullum vobis tempus abibit *iners*, etc.	Ov. *A.A*. III. 60.

The commonest adjectives so used and so placed are *iners*, *miser*, *pius* and *prior*; the following are rarer (the references are not intended to be exhaustive):

biceps (Ov. *F*. I. 230)	minor (Ov. *H*. XIX. 98, 146;
brevis (Ov. *P*. III. 1. 36; IV. 12. 12)	*Tr*. V. 12. 22)
	niger (Ov. *A.A*. I. 724)
ferox (Ov. *P*. I. 2. 124)	probus (Ov. *P*. II. 3. 14)
ferus (Ov. *P*. II. 9. 48)	rudis (Ov. *H*. I. 78)
levis (Ov. *H*. XVII. 2; *A.A*. III. 740; *Tr*. I. 1. 30)	tenax (Ov. *P*. I. 9. 28)
	trux (Ov. *H*. XIX. 144; *P*. IV.
malus (Ov. *P*. III. 2. 20)	6. 32)
vafer (Ov. *H*. XX. 30)	

(2) *Adjectives used substantivally*

Not a few words in Latin are both substantives and adjectives, e.g. *senex*, *anus*; and almost any adjective can be used substantivally with the true substantive understood, e.g. 'bonus (vir)', e.g.

---

[1] = 'having dared to be the first to ask'.

siqua voles apte nubere, nube *pari*   Ov. *H.* IX. 32 (*sc.* 'viro').

Not infrequently the substantive to be understood is mentioned (often in another case) earlier in the pentameter, or in the hexameter, e.g.

victaque concessit prisca *moneta novae*
                               Ov. *F.* I. 222 (*sc.* 'monetae').

reddat, et emendet *facta* priora *novis*
                               Ov. *F.* IV. 596 (*sc.* 'factis').

fert bene praecipites *navis* modo facta procellas;
    quamlibet exiguo solvitur imbre *vetus*
                               Ov. *Tr.* IV. 6. 35–6 (*sc.* 'navis').

nam pudet in geminos ita nomen scindere *versus*,
    desinat ut prior hoc, incipiatque *minor*
                               Ov. *P.* IV. 12. 7–8 (*sc.* 'versus').

In some cases it is not easy to say whether the adjective is being used predicatively or substantivally, e.g.

admoneo veniat ne quis ad illa *loquax*   Ov. *A.A.* II. 608.

(3) *Adjectives necessary to the sense*

Many adjectives which are not in their particular sentence used predicatively are nevertheless essential for the sense of the passage. In other words the conjoined adjective and substantive form a semantic unity in which the idea supplied by the former is as important as that furnished by the latter. For instance, when Lygdamus,[1] wishing to explain that he was born in 43 B.C., says that his birth occurred 'cum cecidit fato consul uterque *pari*', he could not have expressed this fact had he omitted 'pari'; or when Tibullus's drunken lover swears[2] 'that he was mad' ('mente fuisse *mala*'), he could not have done so without the help of the adjective. In such

[1] Tib. (Lygd.) III. 5. 18.   [2] II. 5. 104.

cases, which are not very common, the elegists do not scruple to end the pentameter with the necessary adjective. The commonest adjectives so used are *bonus*,[1] *malus*,[2] *novus*,[3] and *par*;[4] less common are *brevis*,[5] *ferus*,[6] *iners*,[7] and *memor*.[8]

In all the cases so far cited the 'necessity' of the adjective is indisputable; in many others it is not so clearly so, and at the far end of the scale, if one could arrange them in a descending order of necessity, these adjectives would be found to tail off into little more than *epitheta ornantia*. For example when Ovid writes to his wife 'coniugis exemplum diceris esse *bonae*' (*P.* III. 1. 44), the degree of 'necessity' for 'bonae' depends on Ovid's view of the general goodness or otherwise of Roman wives.

(4) *Geographic adjectives*

A few adjectives denoting provenance are allowed to stand last in the pentameter, e.g. 'praebet... | cinnamon... multi pastor odoris *Arabs*' (Prop. III. 13. 7–8); 'nec dedignare maritum | ... *Phrygem*' (Ov. *H.* XVI. 195–6).

(5) *Qualified adjectives*

By these are meant adjectives which, in order to express the author's full meaning, require the quasi-adverbial addition of a substantive, generally in the genitive, dative, or ablative case. Such are not infrequently found ending the pentameter. Examples in Ovid are:

celer	*H.* V. 58.	... ut venias *in mea damna celer*.
frequens	*H.* XVI. 54.	... piceis *ilicibus*que *frequens*.

[1] e.g. Prop. I. 10. 28; Ov. *Am.* I. 10. 48; *Tr.* I. 6. 26.
[2] e.g. Prop. II. 9. 22; Ov. *H.* XIII. 86.
[3] e.g. Ov. *H.* XVII. 144; *F.* V. 678.
[4] e.g. Prop. III. 9. 38; Ov. *F.* V. 704.
[5] Ov. *H.* VII. 188. [6] Ov. *R.A.* 656.
[7] Ov. *P.* I. 5. 44. [8] Prop. II. 13. 40.

gravis	*H.* X. 138.	et tunicas *lacrimis* sicut ab imbre *gravis*.
inops	*A.A.* III. 684.	nec sis audita paelice *mentis inops*.
memor	*P.* III. 1. 146.	fac sis *personae*, quam tueare, *memor*.
minax	*Tr.* I. 2. 24.	fluctibus hic tumidus, *nubibus* ille *minax*.
minor[1]	*Tr.* V. 6. 42.	crede mihi, *vero* est nostra querella *minor*.
par[2]	*Tr.* V. 12. 30.	*illi*, qui fueram, posse redire *parem*.
rudis	*Tr.* II. 424.	Ennius ingenio maximus, *arte rudis*.
	P. III. 7. 18.	*ad mala* iampridem non sumus ulla *rudes*.
	F. IV. 335–6.	. . .iuvencam
		mactarunt *operum coniugii*que *rudem*.
sacer	*F.* III. 264.	est locus antiqua *religione sacer*.

(6) *Present participles*

These may be used in Latin substantivally, adjectivally, and participially, e.g. *amans*, 'a lover'; *amans maritus*, 'a loving husband'; *pater liberos amans*, 'a father who loves his children'. Strictly speaking only the adjectival use concerns us here; but it may be convenient to consider all three uses together. Nine different participles are found at the end of pentameters:

amans. Propertius has one substantival example, 'tota nocte receptus *amans*' (II. 14. 28); Ovid has ten[3] or eleven.[4]

decens. Propertius has one adjectival instance, 'Cynthia. . . furibunda *decens*' (IV. 8. 52), 'lovely in her fury'; and Ovid two, 'forma sine arte *decens*' (*R.A.* 350), and 'culta versicolore *decens*' (*F.* V. 356), in both of which cases the

[1] Particularly common in Ovid, e.g. also *H.* IX. 30; *Tr.* II. 112; V. 2. 50; V. 6. 42; *P.* I. 2. 76; I. 9. 38; II. 2. 74; III. 1. 94.

[2] See also Ov. *H.* III. 32; *Tr.* III. 7. 40; *P.* IV. 13. 12.

[3] *Am.* I. 8. 78; I. 9. 2; I. 9. 10; III. 6. 22; *H.* IV. 154; XI. 126; XVIII. 56; *A.A.* I. 502; III. 554; *R.A.* 36.

[4] The dubious case is 'nunquam. . .cruoris *amans*' (*P.* II. 9. 46). Palmer in his edition of the *Heroides* (on XIII. 110) regards this as a participle; Owen in his edition of *Tristia* II (on l. 358) as an adjective. Considering the genitive, I should have thought it was a substantive.

participial adjective is qualified by an ablative and both might be considered as coming under (5) above.

egens. Only 'semper amet, fructu semper amoris *egens*' (Prop. III. 20. 30), where it is difficult to say whether the word is an adjective or a true participle.

favens. Only 'horaque conveniens auspiciumque *favens*' (Ov. P. III. 1. 160), where the participle is clearly used adjectivally.[1]

(?) *ferens.* At Ov. *Tr.* II. 357–8 the *codd. dett.* offer 'voluptas | plurima mulcendis auribus apta *ferens*'. If this reading is correct, we get an instance, as Owen (*op. cit.*) points out, the only instance in Ovid, of a real participial use at the end of the pentameter. Owen himself accepts the reading 'feres'.

(?) *fremens.* At Ov. *F.* III. 633–4 some editors (e.g. Merkel, Peter) accept the reading 'Lavinia volnus | mente premit tacita dissimulatque *fremens*'. Again, if this be what Ovid really wrote, we find a true participle at the end of the pentameter. Most editors, however, adopt the alternative reading 'metus'.

latens.[2] Only 'Lygdamus ad plutei fulcra sinistra *latens* | eruitur' (Prop. IV. 8. 68–9); a clear participial use.

nocens. Ovid has one adjectival use, 'quaeque iuvet, monstrat, quaeque sit herba *nocens*' (*Tr.* II. 270), where the adjective is a predicate. He has six[3] cases in which 'nocens' is substantival (='a criminal'), e.g. 'acceptum refero versibus esse *nocens*' (*Tr.* II. 10).

potens. Only 'forma sine arte *potens*' (Ov. *A.A.* III. 258), where the participle is used as a qualified adjective.

[1] Regarded by Palmer, in his note on *H.* XIII. 110, as a participle—surely wrongly after the 'adsit' of the hexameter.

[2] Palmer's attempt to introduce 'latens' in place of 'tuis' at the end of Ov. *H.* XIII. 110 was rightly castigated by Housman, *C.R.* XIII (1899), p. 174 *b*.

[3] *Am.* II. 19. 14; *H.* IV. 28; XII. 106; XII. 132; *Tr.* II. 10; *P.* II. 10. 12.

sedens. Only '...sertisque sepulchrum | ornabit custos ad mea busta *sedens*' (Prop. III. 16. 23–4); a true participle.

sequens. Only 'dicere non norunt quid ferat hora *sequens*' (Tib. (Lygd.) III. 4. 46).

In tabulated form:

	Substantival	Adjectival	Participial
Tib. I and II	–	–	–
Tib. (Lygd.)	–	1	–
Propertius	1	1 or 2	2 or 3
Ovid	17	5	?2

(7) '*Epitheta ornantia*'

Much the commonest of these is *novus*, which occurs as last word in the pentameter about forty times in the elegists. As was said above, no hard and fast line can be drawn between the 'necessary' and the 'ornamental' use of this adjective. For instance, when Ovid writes 'membraque sunt cera pallidiora *nova*' (*P.* I. 10. 28), he might perhaps have omitted the adjective without detriment to the sense of the line, though, as wax darkens with age, the addition of 'nova' does add point.

Next in order of frequency is *pius*, which Ovid allows to stand at the end of the pentameter some dozen times, e.g. 'officium...*pium*' (*Tr.* III. 3. 84); 'flammae...*piae*' (*F.* VI. 440).

Other, rarer, adjectives so found are:

brevis	Ov. *H.* XIV. 128.	sculptaque sint titulo nostra sepulchra *brevi*.
cavus[1]	Prop. IV. 5. 68.	sputaque per dentes ire cruenta *cavos*.
	Ov. *Am.* III. 8. 40.	...in quercu mella reperta *cava*.
gravis	Prop. II. 29. 16.	...oculos moverit illa *gravis*.

[1] Both these examples may be regarded as 'necessary'.

47

levis	Prop. I. 9. 32.	nedum tu possis, spiritus iste *levis*.
	Prop. IV. 2. 43–4.	. . .cucurbita. . . me notat et iunco brassica vincta *levi*.
	Ov. *P.* IV. 16. 30.	et tua cum socco Musa, Melisse, *levi*.
memor	Prop. II. 13. 40.	. . .ad lapides. . .*memores*.
	Ov. *F.* VI. 78.	. . .posteritasque *memor*?
minax	Prop. III. 10. 6.	ponat et in sicco molliter unda *minax*.
nobilis	Prop. I. 11. 3–4.	mirantem subdita. . . . . .Misenis aequora *nobilibus*.
purpureus	Tib. (Lygd.) III. 4. 30.	et color in niveo corpore *purpureus*.[1]
rudis	Ov. *A.A.* II. 220.	creditur et lanas excoluisse *rudes*.
sacer	Tib. II. 5. 90.	. . .flammas. . .*sacras*.
	Tib. II. 5. 114.	. . .vati. . .*sacro*.
salax	Ov. *A.A.* II. 422.	bulbus et, ex horto quae venit, herba *salax*.[2]
supplex	Prop. I. 16. 3–4.	. . .limina. . . captorum lacrimis umida *supplicibus*.
trux	Ov. *H.* IV. 166.	. . .eris tauro saevior ipse *truci*?
uber	Prop. I. 22. 9–10.	. . .Umbria. . . me genuit terris fertilis *uberibus*.

[1] This comes very near to being a 'necessary' epithet.
[2] Almost 'necessary'.

(d) PENTAMETERS WITH INTERNAL RHYME

Pentameters in which the last word of the first half rhymes with the last word of the second half, e.g. 'prodita sunt *facto*, nomina cara, *meo*' (Ov. *H.* X. 70), are found in all the elegists on an average which scarcely varies between them. For instance, Tib. I and II show internal rhyme in 20% of pentameters, Tib. (Lygd.) in 21%, *Corp. Tib.* in 24%, Prop. I and II in 23%, Ov. *R.A.* in 23%, and Ov. *Tr.* II in 20·4%.

In about 90% of the cases the rhyme, like the one quoted above, is between a substantive and an adjective in agreement. S. G. Owen in his note on Ov. *Tr.* II. 104 implies that these rhymes were intentional, but a cursory inspection of any of the poems shows that Ovid often failed to rhyme where he could easily have done so; e.g. at *H.* VII. 50; VIII. 94; IX. 60; IX. 148, an opening dactyl without rhyme is preferred to rhyme with an opening spondee. (This short passage from the *Heroides* was taken for examination at random.)

A still less likely theory is that of Eichner, *De poetarum latinorum distichis quaestionum metricarum particulae duae* (Sorau Diss., 1866), who holds that the elegiac couplet is divisible into four sections: (*a*) the first 'half' of the hexameter as far as the third-foot caesura, (*b*) the second 'half' of the hexameter after the third-foot caesura, (*c*) the first half of the pentameter, and (*d*) the second half of the pentameter. Of these, according to Eichner, any two are intentionally written so as to correspond both by homoeoteleuton and metrically, e.g.

> ibit ad adfect*am*, ⋮ quae non languebit, amic*am*:
>   vīsăt, ĕt | ĭndĭcĭ|*īs* ‖ aēgră sĭt | ĭllă tŭ|*īs*.
>
> Ov. *Am.* II. 2. 21–2.

CHAPTER IV

Prosody

(a) INDETERMINATE VOWEL QUANTITY

Occasionally the same word is found in the elegists with a vowel, or with vowels of different (A) quantity, or (B) kind.

A. These quantitatively differing vowels may be found (1) open at the end of the word, or (2) closed or medial.

(1) -ĕ.[1]

The only instance of this is 'cavĕ'. Propertius always has 'cavĕ'; Ovid writes both -ĕ and -ē, but the former seems to be confined to prohibitions, e.g. 'tu cavĕ defendas' (*Tr.* I. I. 25), but 'cognatum fratremque cavē carumque sodalem' (*A.A.* I. 753; cf. *Tr.* I. I. 87).

-ŏ.[2]

(a) *Substantives, pronouns, and numerals*

nemŏ. Long in *Corp. Tib.* III. 13. 8, the only instance. Propertius also has 'nemō' once (II. 19. 32); in all his other instances[3] the final vowel is elided. Ovid has 'nemō' in *Am.* I. 8. 100; *Tr.* I. 9. 44; *P.* III. 6. 58, but 'nemŏ' in *Am.* I. 8. 43; *Tr.* II. 348; *P.* II. 3. 16 (if genuine); *F.* VI. 324. It may be no more than a coincidence that 'nemō' occurs only at the end of the first half of the pentameter.

egŏ. '"egŏ" is the invariable scansion in classical poetry' (Lindsay, *The Latin Language*, p. 422). The only apparent

---

[1] For -ē shortened before a vowel, see p. 59.
[2] See R. Hartenberger, *De 'o' finali apud poetas latinos* (Bonn Diss., 1911).
[3] II. 14. 18; II. 16. 19; II. 30. 25; II. 30. 31; II. 34. 3; III. 16. 14.

exception is 'Tuscus egō Tuscis orior' (Prop. IV. 2. 3), where the *codd. dett.* give 'ego et Tuscis'—a reading adopted, rightly, by Butler and Barber.

leŏ. 'leŏ' (Ov. *A.A.* I. 762). None of the poets has 'leō' in elegiacs, though it occurs in Ovid's[1] hexameter poem, the *Halieuticon*: 'impiger, ecce, leō venantum sternere pergit' (l. 52).

homŏ. The final *-o* was originally long[2] but became short under the influence of the *lex breves breviantes*.[3] The word occurs only once in the elegists, and there (Ov. *Ibis* 408) the *-o* is short.

duŏ. Always *-ŏ* in the elegists.

ambŏ. Always *-ō* in the elegists.

Besides these common nouns Ovid allows himself to shorten, for metrical purposes, the following proper names:

Curiŏ	*F.* II. 527
Galliŏ	*P.* IV. 11. 1
Nasŏ	*Am.* I. 11. 27 and *passim*
Scipiŏ	*A.A.* III. 410
Semŏ	*F.* VI. 214
Sulmŏ	*Am.* II. 16. 1; *Tr.* IV. 10. 3

(*b*) *Verbs*

(i) The final *-o* of the first person singular of the present indicative: this vowel is usually, and was originally, long; but in a few verbs it is sometimes found short in the elegiac writers. These are mostly disyllabic, and, where the first

---

[1] If indeed Ovid be the author (see B. Axelson in *Eranos* XLIII, 1945, pp. 23–35).

[2] Kühner, *Ausführliche Grammatik der lateinischen Sprache* (Hanover, 1912–14), I. p. 113.

[3] The philological law by which words originally of iambic scansion (hence the German word for it—*Iambenkürzungsgesetz*) became pyrrhics, e.g. *mĭhī* became *mĭhĭ*.

syllable is short, have been influenced by the *lex breves breviantes*. In Propertius are found: 'volŏ' (II. 10. 9), 'putŏ' (II. 26. 18,[1] parenthetic), 'findŏ' (III. 9. 35);[2] in Ovid 'putŏ' (24 cases of -ŏ and ten of -ō (end of pentameter); indeed -ō is never found either used parenthetically, as at *Am.* I. 2. 5, or as part of the construction, as at *Tr.* I. 1. 44; *P.* II. 7. 20), 'negŏ' (*Am.* I. 10. 64), 'volŏ' (*Am.* II. 5. 54), 'tollŏ' (*Am.* III. 2. 26), 'amŏ' (*Am.* III. 14. 39, if genuine; *R.A.* 648), 'rogŏ' (*H.* XI. 127),[3] 'petŏ' (*H.* XVI. 35, etc.), 'sciŏ' (*Tr.* V. 4. 46), 'credŏ' (*P.* I. 7. 56), 'canŏ' (*P.* III. 9. 35).

Trisyllabic verbs:[4] 'desinŏ' (Tib. II. 6. 41; Ov. *H.* XVIII. 203), 'conferŏ' (Ov. *P.* I. 1. 25).

(ii) The final -*o* of the future or future perfect: 'erŏ' (Ov. *Tr.* IV. 10. 130), 'oderŏ' (Ov. *Am.* III. 11. 35), 'dabŏ' (Ov. *H.* XVII. 260).

(iii) The final -*o* of the imperative:[5] 'caeditŏ' (Prop. IV. 5. 77, *nisi leg.* 'caedite'), 'estŏ' (Ov. *Tr.* IV. 3. 72), but 'estō' (Ov. *H.* XX. 66).

(c) *Conjunctions, adverbs, etc.*

ergŏ. This word, being nothing but the Greek ἔργῳ, has -ō always in Tibullus and Propertius, except for one case in each poet where it is elided. Ovid, except where he elides, always has -ō except at *H.* V. 59 and *Tr.* I. 1. 87, where 'ergŏ' is found.

---

[1] 'qui, put(ŏ), Arioniam vexerat ante lyram.' Were this -ō, we should have a violation of the rule forbidding the elision of a cretic (see p. 73).

[2] Housman (*J. of Phil.* XXI, p. 160) calls this 'the earliest example in Latin poetry of a spondee transformed into a trochee by the shortening of a final *o*'.

[3] Used parenthetically. I see no reason for suspecting this reading; see Housman in *C.R.* XIII (1899), p. 173.

[4] In Ov. *H.* XV. 32, Bentley's 'repende' must be accepted for the impossible 'rependŏ' of the MSS. (so Palmer).

[5] 'medicandŏ' (Tib. III. 6. 3) and 'tegendŏ' (Ov. *H.* IX. 126) are impossible readings.

quando, ecquando, quandocumque, aliquando, adeo, ideo, idcirco
are always -ō in the elegists; compounds of *modŏ* (*dummodo,
postmodo*) always -ŏ.

(2) -ă̆-.

'Ārabius', 'Ārabia' (Prop. I. 14. 19; II. 3. 15; II. 10. 16),
but 'Ărabs', 'Ărabum' (Prop. II. 29. 17; III. 13. 8: Ov. *H.*
XV. 76).

-ĕ̆-.

'chorēis' (Prop. I. 3. 5), but 'chorĕas' (Prop. II. 19. 15).

The normal scansion of the second person singular of *esse*
is *ĕs*, but at Prop. II. 32. 61 the MSS. offer '...tuque ēs
imitata Latinas'. Despite Rothstein's defence this is impossible, though, as Butler and Barber remark, *ēs* is not uncommon
in Plautus.

A good many instances occur in the elegists of the third
person plural of the perfect tense ending in -ĕrunt instead of
the normal -ērunt. Tibullus has 'profuĕrunt' (II. 3. 12) and
'dedĕrunt' (III. 11. 4); Propertius[1] 'contulĕrunt' (II. 3. 25),
and Ovid:

audiĕrunt	*F.* III. 65	molliĕrunt	*Am.* II. 1. 22
compulĕrunt	*F.* III. 860	praebuĕrunt	*Am.* I. 14. 25;
contigĕrunt	*F.* I. 592		*H.* II. 142
excidĕrunt	*H.* XII. 71	profuĕrunt	*R.A.* 263
expulĕrunt	*H.* XIV. 72	quaesiĕrunt	*H.* V. 136
fuĕrunt	*A.A.* III. 405	stetĕrunt	*H.* VII. 166
horruĕrunt	*F.* II. 502	terruĕrunt	*Am.* III. 5. 2
imbuĕrunt	*Ibis* 229	vagiĕrunt	*F.* II. 405

[1] If Scaliger's emendations be accepted, there are four more Propertian
instances: 'fuĕrunt' (I. 11. 29), 'stetĕrunt' (II. 8. 10), 'excidĕrunt' (III. 24. 20;
IV. 7. 15). In all these lines the MSS. give pluperfects. See Butler and Barber
ad locc., and Housman in *Proceedings of the Classical Association*, 1921,
pp. 82 sqq.

It will be noticed that eleven out of these seventeen instances
are words which with the normal scansion would be impossible in elegiacs.[1]

$-\breve{\imath}-.$[2]

'ullīus' (Ov. *Tr.* II. 112; 564), but 'ullĭus' (Ov. *Tr.* v.
6. 34).

'unīus' (Ov. *A.A.* I. 688), but 'unĭus' (Ov. *Am.* I.
13. 20).

'illīus' (Ov. *Am.* I. 13. 44), but 'illĭus' (Ov. *Am.*
I. 4. 34).

'Īōnia' (Prop. I. 6. 31; Ov. *F.* VI. 175; and 'Īōniacas', Ov.
H. IX. 73), but 'Īŏnius', etc. (Prop. II. 26. 2; III. 11. 72; Ov.
Tr. I. 4. 3; *P.* IV. 5. 6).

'Dīana'[3] (Prop. II. 28. 60), but elsewhere in the elegists
'Dĭana' (e.g. Prop. II. 19. 17; IV. 8. 29).

$-\breve{o}-.$

'Īōnia', 'Īŏnius': see above.

'Sidōnia' (Prop. II. 16. 55; Ov. *P.* I. 3. 77), but elsewhere
'Sidŏnius' (e.g. Tib. III. 3. 18; Prop. II. 29. 15; Ov. *Tr.*
IV. 3. 2).

'Ōrion' (Prop. II. 16. 51; Ov. *A.A.* I. 731), but 'Ŏrion'
(Prop. II. 26. 56; Ov. *A.A.* II. 56).

[1] On the form *-ĕrunt* see Lindsay, *op. cit.* p. 532, Kühner, *op. cit.* I, p. 672–3,
Stolz-Schmalz (fifth ed. Leumann-Hofmann), p. 338. (The latter regard *-ērunt*
as a contamination of *-ĕrunt* and *-ēre*.) Lindsay and Kühner say, without
evidence, that *-ĕrunt* was colloquial. Plautus uses *-ĕrunt* only at the end of
a line or hemistich; neither Ennius nor the tragedians use it at all, and Lucretius
has no more than a few examples (see Monro on I. 406).

[2] For 'sanguĭs' see p. 59 n. 3; for *-erĭs*, the termination of the future
perfect indicative and the perfect subjunctive, see note at the end of this
chapter; for 'nihĭl' see p. 61.

[3] See 'Dīana' (Virg. *Aen.* I. 499), though elsewhere in that poet 'Dĭana';
doubtless originally *ī* ('dea Iana'); later shortened before the following *a*.

-ŭ-.

'Lŭceres' (Prop. IV. 1. 31), but 'Lūceribus' (Ov. *F.* III. 132).

'Mamūr(r)ius' (Prop. IV. 2. 61), but 'Mamŭrius' (Ov. *F.* III. 389, 392).

Such variants as 'Ātrides' (e.g. Prop. III. 18. 30; Ov. *Am.* I. 9. 37) and 'Ătrides' (e.g. Prop. II. 14. 1; Ov. *R.A.* 779), 'Ētruscus' (e.g. Prop. I. 21. 2) and 'Ĕtruscus' (e.g. Prop. I. 22. 6), 'Ferētri' (Prop. IV. 10. 45) and 'Ferĕtri' (*ib.* 48) are, of course, not cases of indeterminate vowel quantity but merely of the use or non-use of 'epic lengthening' before mute and liquid.[1]

B. The only change of vowel is that between *-ĕ* and *-ī*.

(1) The following ablatives, of which the normal termination is *-ī*, are sometimes found in Ovid ending in *-ĕ*:

bimestre	*F.* VI. 158
caeleste	*H.* XVI. 277
consorte	*F.* III. 873
inerte	*P.* I. 5. 8; I. 10. 14
marĕ	*A.A.* III. 94; *Tr.* V. 2. 20; *P.* IV. 6. 46
parĕ[2]	*F.* III. 193; III. 526; IV. 98
perenne	*H.* VIII. 64; *F.* III. 654
rivalĕ	*Am.* I. 8. 95; I. 9. 18: *R.A.* 791
sollerte	*P.* IV. 14. 35

(2) The adverb *here* (*heri*) is found in the form 'herĕ' when it is not the final word in the line, e.g. 'scis herĕ me...' (Prop. II. 22. 1); 'scis herĕ te...' (Ov. *Am.* I. 8. 23); 'hic herĕ Phrixeae...' (Ov. *F.* III. 852); but 'herī' at the end of the pentameter, e.g. Prop. II. 14. 20; III. 23. 12; Ov. *F.* II. 76. Quintilian (I. 7. 22) calls *here* the modern, *heri* the old, form, and further remarks (I. 4. 8) 'in *here* neque E plane neque I auditur'.

---

[1] Cf. 'sive săcro pavi, sedive sub arbore săcra' (Ov. *F.* IV. 749).

[2] Cf. 'compare' (*Am.* III. 5. 38; *A.A.* III. 359).

NOTE ON THE TERMINATIONS (-ER*Ĭ*S, -ER*Ĭ*TIS) OF THE FUTURE PERFECT INDICATIVE AND PERFECT SUBJUNCTIVE

It is fairly certain that originally the -*eris* of the future perfect indicative (which is no more than the future of *sum* appended as an auxiliary verb)[1] had a short *i*. That of the perfect subjunctive, on the other hand (being an optative formation),[2] had a long one. The whole question has been exhaustively treated by Owen in his note on *Tr.* II. 323. He concludes: 'in poetical language the two terminations were early confounded, and the ending in either case is treated indifferently as long or short.'

Propertius has three instances[3] of -*erĭs* in the future perfect, one[4] of -*erĭs* in the perfect subjunctive, and one[5] of -*erīs* in the future perfect.

In Ovid the figures are: fut. perf. -*erĭs*, ten instances; fut. perf. -*erīs*, sixteen instances; perf. subj. -*erĭs*, one instance (*Tr.* II. 323), and perf. subj. -*erīs*, nine instances.

A similar uncertainty marks the quantity of the penultimate *i* of the second[6] person plural of these two tenses. It is normally short, but in at least two lines of Ovid it is found long:

et maris Ionii transierītis aquas	*P.* IV. 5. 6.
consulis, ut limen contigerītis, erit	*P.* IV. 5. 16.

---

[1] Lindsay, *op. cit.* p. 510.

[2] Kühner, *op. cit.* I, p. 116; Lindsay, *op. cit.* p. 500; Stolz-Schmalz[5], who point out (p. 340) that the distinction between the optative and future perfect forms was still observed by Plautus and Ennius, while later writers used the two forms indifferently as metrical needs dictated.

[3] III. 10. 19; IV. 1. 141 (?); IV. 5. 33.

[4] II. 30. 33 (so Owen on Ov. *Tr.* II. 323).   [5] II. 15. 50.

[6] *ī* is sometimes found in the first person plural, e.g. 'fecerīmus' (Cat. v. 10), but no instances of this occur in the elegists.

(b) HIATUS AND VOWEL LENGTHENING

1. *Hiatus*

By hiatus is meant the non-elision of a final open vowel or
-*m* before an initial vowel. There are three types:

    (i) hiatus after interjections;
    (ii) hiatus at a caesura (generally the third);
    (iii) Greek hiatus.

(i) Hiatus is constantly found in the elegists after the
interjections *o*, *heu*, and *a*, e.g.

o | ego, cum aspicerem...	Tib. II. 3. 5.
a, | ego, ne possim...	Tib. III. 4. 82.
tuque, o | Eurytion...	Prop. II. 33. 31.
egerat a stabulis, o | Erythea, tuis...	Prop. IV. 9. 2.
o | utinam arguerem...[1]	Ov. *Am.* II. 5. 7.
o | in corde meo...	*ib.* II. 9. 2.
o | argumenti...	*ib.* III. 1. 16.
o | ita, Phoebe, velis...	Ov. *A.A.* III. 347.
heu, | ubi Mars pater est?	Ov. *F.* v. 465.

(ii) Instances of caesural hiatus are almost always confused
by textual considerations. The reading of some MSS. shows
hiatus, that of others shows none. The problem is this: Has
MS. corruption caused an apparent hiatus where the poet did
not make one, or did the poet, relying on the metrical pause
and (often) a break in the sense also, allow himself a hiatus
which a 'learned' copyist has 'emended'? No general rule
can be laid down, and cases must be decided (if they can be
decided) on their respective merits. All that can be done is
to cite the instances. They are:

    et, tantum venerata virum, \| hunc sedula curet   Tib. I. 5. 33.

[1] Very frequent in Ovid.

(Some MSS. give the meaningless 'nunc' for 'hunc'.)

    ite, rates curvae, | et leti texite causas   Prop. III. 7. 29.

(Butler and Barber accept Passerat's 'curvas'.)

    o me felicem! | o nox mihi candida! et o tu   Prop. II. 15. 1.

(The correct reading of this line is much disputed. Some MSS. give 'nox o mihi', a reading to which Butler and Barber incline, though they give 'o nox mihi' in the text.)

    haec eadem ante illam | impune et Lesbia fecit   Prop. II. 32. 45.

(Some MSS. give '...illam iam impune...'.)

    sed Chio thalamo | aut Oricia terebintho   Prop. III. 7. 49.

(Possibly a conscious adaptation of Virgil's 'buxo | aut Oricia terebintho', *Aen.* X. 136.)

    Castor(i) Amyclaeo | et Amyclaeo Polluci   Ov. *H.* VIII. 71.

(Palmer rightly regards this line as spurious; see p. 73 n. 3.)

    forsitan et pulsa | Aetolide Deianira   Ov. *H.* IX. 131.

('The word *Aetolide* is perhaps corrupt', Palmer.)

    (iii) Of this type of hiatus Palmer (app. I, p. 509) says: 'Ovid often uses hiatus in the fifth arsis; but almost always under two conditions, (1) that the second word is a proper name, (2) that the first word is an adjective in agreement with it.' There are nine instances, all in Ovid:

arsit et Oenides in Maenalia	Atalanta	*H.* IV. 99.
ut Tegeaeus aper cupressifero	Erymantho	*H.* IX. 87.
Eurytidosque Ioles atque Aonii	Alcidae	*H.* IX. 133.

semivir occubuit in lotifero | Eueno	*H.* IX. 141.
ille Noto Zephyroque et Sithonio | Aquiloni[1]	*H.* XI. 13.
quid fuit asperius Nonacrina | Atalanta	*A.A.* II. 185.
si scelere Oeclides Talaioniae | Eriphylae	*A.A.* III. 13.
Amphiareïades Naupactoo | Acheloo	*F.* II. 43.
hinc sata Pleïone cum caelifero | Atlante[2]	*F.* V. 83.

We may here add two instances of another Graecism, viz. the shortening, in hiatus, of an open long vowel at the end of a word before an initial long vowel:

Omphalĕ \| in tantum formae processit honorem

Prop. III. 11. 17.

lenis ades, precibusque meis favĕ \| Ilithyia

Ov. *Am.* II. 13. 21.

2. *Vowel lengthening*

Closely related to hiatus is the not infrequent practice of the elegists of lengthening a naturally short, closed[3] final syllable before an initial vowel. This lengthening occurs almost always at the main caesura of the hexameter or pentameter. As with hiatus there is often MS. uncertainty.

Tib. I and II show three[4] cases:

at si tardus erīs | errabis. transiet aetas	I. 4. 27.
nunc ad bella trahōr, | et iam quis forsitan hostis	I. 10. 13.
ipse suos Geniūs | adsit visurus honores	II. 2. 5.

[1] 'Greek' hiatus applied to a non-Greek word.

[2] Cf. p. 11, n. 5.

[3] Housman has shown (*C.Q.* XXI, 1927, pp. 2–11) that the following lines, all of which show lengthened -ă at the main caesura, all need correction: Tib. I. 7. 61; Prop. II. 13. 25; II. 29. 39; IV. 5. 64: Ov. *Am.* III. 7. 55.

[4] 'quidquid agit sanguĭs \| est tamen illa tuus' (Tib. I. 6. 66) is not a case, for the ĭ of *sanguis* was originally long (see Lindsay, *op. cit.* p. 377; and Stolz-Schmalz[5], p. 264, who postulate an early form *sanguins*); cf. 'educet: at sanguĭs \| ille sororis erat' (Ov. *F.* VI. 488). For the commoner *sanguĭs* see, e.g., Ov. *Am.* I. 7. 60.

PROSODY

There is one in *Corp. Tib.*:

> hoc Venus ignoscēt: | at tu, violente, caveto   III. 8. 3.

In Propertius occur:

> neu, siquid petiĭt, | ingrata fronte negaris   I. 10. 23.
> vinceris aut vincīs, | haec in amore rota est   II. 8. 8.
> cui fugienda fuĭt | indocti semita vulgi   II. 23. 1.

(This is actually an emendation of Housman's accepted by Butler and Barber. The MSS. give 'cui fuit indocti fugienda et...'.)

> aut pudor ingenuūs, | aut reticendus amor   II. 24. 4.

(Butler and Barber accept Haupt's 'ingenuis'.)

> et tibi Maeonias inter | heroidas omnis   II. 28. 29.

(Other MSS. 'omnes heroidas inter', probably rightly: cf. 'sanctas heroidas inter', Ov. *Tr.* I. 6. 33.)

> nulli cura fuĭt | externos quaerere divos   IV. 1. 17.

With perhaps two[1] exceptions, 'utinam vivāt | et' (*Tr.* V. 7. 23) and 'Hyadās | aut' (*F.* III. 105), all the Ovidian instances conform to one type: they all show the lengthening of the ĭ in the third person singular of the perfect indicative of verbs forming their perfect in -*ii* (mainly compounds of *eo*). The forms in question are: 'abiit',[2] 'adiit',[3] 'periit',[4] 'petiit',[5] 'praeteriit',[6] 'rediit',[7] and 'subiit'.[8] In two instances Ovid

---

[1] 'occubuĭt' (*H.* IX. 141) is corrupt.
[2] *H.* XV. 173; *F.* III. 474; IV. 721.   [3] *P.* I. 3. 74.
[4] *Am.* III. 8. 17; *H.* XIX. 128; *Tr.* III. 14. 36; IV. 3. 68; *Ibis* 341, 369, 530; *P.* IV. 12. 44.
[5] *Am.* III. 5. 30.   [6] *A.A.* III. 63–4.
[7] *H.* VI. 31 (Heinsius); XIII. 29; *A.A.* III. 707; *R.A.* 6; *F.* II. 341; III. 333; V. 515.
[8] *P.* I. 4. 46.

60

converts a natural tribrach not into an anapaest but into an iambus:

...pĕtīt, | auctoris...	*Tr.* I. 10. 25.
...pĕtīt | altum...	*F.* I. 109.

Of this lengthening of the *ĭ* two explanations are possible. According to Palmer[1] 'Ovid freely lengthens perfects of verbs otherwise forming a tribrach.... He evidently admitted these lengthenings in accordance with the rule which permitted poets to alter the quantity of words which otherwise could not come into verse (as proper names in Greek tragedy): for whereas he has been far more liberal in lengthening the final syllable in tribrachs in *-it* than Virgil or Horace, he is far more rigid than Virgil in forbidding caesural lengthening in the case of words which could be brought into the verse without it.' The weak point in this explanation is that these natural tribrachs are perfectly possible, and indeed constantly found, in verse. The poet had only to see to it that they were followed by a word beginning with a consonant.

The more likely explanation is that Ovid allows himself to return, *metri gratia*, to the older vowel quantity,[2] *ī*, in much the same way as a Victorian poet would write 'wreath'd' or the older 'wreathéd' according as either suited his metre, or (a nearer parallel) 'wĭnd' or 'wīnd' as either suited his rhyme.

To these verbal instances may be added two cases in which the final syllable of *nihil* stands long before a vowel:

morte nihīl opus est   Ov. *Tr.* V. 14. 41; *P.* III. 1. 113.

This syllable, originally long,[3] was shortened by the *lex breves breviantes*.

[1] *Op. cit.* pp. 327–8.
[2] As with *sanguis*; see above, p. 59, and Lindsay, *op. cit.* pp. 527–8.
[3] Kühner, *op. cit.* p. 118; see Housman in *C.Q.* x (1916), pp. 138–9.

'reppuleris' (e.g. Ov. *H.* xx. 177), 'rettulerat' (e.g. *ib.* I. 38), etc., are correctly so written, and not 'rēpuleris', 'rētulerat', since these are syncopated forms of the reduplicated perfects, 'rep(e)puleris', 'ret(e)tulerat'. These perfect stems, therefore, have the *e* always long by position.[1]

NOTE ON SHORT OPEN VOWELS BEFORE
SC-, *SM*-, *SP*-, *ST*-, AND *Z*-

Generally speaking short open vowels may not stand before *sc*-, *sm*-, *sp*-, *st*-, or *z*-, but the elegists, like the writers of hexameters, allow themselves the Greek licence of occasionally (1) keeping such final vowels short, or, more rarely, (2) lengthening them before the double consonant.

(1) If words starting with such double consonants take the form of, or begin with, an iambus, it is clear that, without the licence of leaving the preceding short open vowel short, they could not appear in the elegiac metre at all. This fact may in part explain the usage. The cases are:

potiusquĕ smaragdi	Tib. I. I. 51.
viridesquĕ smaragdos	Tib. II. 4. 27.
quoscumquĕ smaragdos	Prop. II. 16. 43.
hebetarĕ smaragdos	Ov. *Am.* II. 6. 21.
cum prolĕ Scamandro[2]	Prop. III. I. 27.
consuluitquĕ striges	Prop. IV. 5. 17.
altă Zacynthos	Ov. *H.* I. 87.

But this excuse cannot be pleaded in the case of:[3]

bracchiă spectavi	Prop. III. II. 53.

[1] Lindsay, *op. cit.* pp. 503–4.

[2] If Wolff's bold conjecture be accepted, as it is by Butler and Barber. Cf. 'unda Scamandri' (Cat. LXIV. 357).

[3] Hilberg (*Wortstellung*, p. 3) gives a list of 23 cases in Ovid where, at least in certain MSS., an open vowel stands short before (mostly) trochaic

nunc ubĭ Scipiadae	Prop. III. 11. 67.
venumdată Scylla figura	Prop. III. 19. 21.
iam benĕ spondebant	Prop. IV. 1. 41.
tu capĕ spinosi	Prop. IV. 4. 48.

(2) There is only one[1] real case of this, since, 'famē stimu-lante' (Tib. I. 5. 53) shows merely the usual ablative of *fames*, which, the word being a heteroclite third and fifth declension substantive, is in -ē.[2] The case is 'pro segetē spicas' (Tib. I. 5. 28). An analogous, and very strange, Tibullan example of the lengthening of an open short vowel before two consonants is 'servarē, frustra' (I. 6. 34).[3]

For a case of lengthening before mute and liquid *within* the word see 'rēgressus' (Ov. *A.A.* II. 32). This word is not found elsewhere in the elegists, but Virgil has 'rĕgressus' (*Aen.* XI. 413).[4]

---

words of the type of 'scripta', but justifiable excision or emendation has removed all these from the pages of Ehwald and Ehwald-Levy except 'strataque Cretaeam belua *stravit* humum' (*H.* X. 106). Palmer rightly accepts here Bentley's 'planxit'.

[1] One, that is to say, in elegiacs. Ovid's contemporary, Grattius, in his *Cynegetica* (hexameters) has 'proceris generosā stirpibus arbor' (l. 142, *nisi leg.* generosam) and 'vulpinā species' (l. 259).

[2] Kühner, *op. cit.* I, p. 486. For an Ovidian instance see 'utque rapax stimulante famē cupidusque cruore' (*Tr.* I. 6. 9).

[3] Cf. 'impotentiā freta' (Cat. IV. 18), etc.

[4] See p. 55.

NOTE ON VOWEL SHORTENING

The shortening of a naturally long vowel before another vowel *in the same word* is perfectly regular, e.g. 'dĕ(h)iscit' (Ov. *Tr.* V. 12. 27), and Ovid extends this use even to the shortening of diphthongs, e.g. 'praĕeunt' (*F.* I. 81). Another possible instance (though the reading is very uncertain) is 'Maĕotis' (Ov. *Tr.* III. 12. 2).[1]

(c) SHORT OPEN VOWELS AT THE END OF THE PENTAMETER

Leaving out of account 'egŏ' and the dative singular of the personal pronouns (whose final *i* is *anceps*), all of which words are often found last in the pentameter, the figures and percentages for pentameters ending in a short open vowel are as follows:

	Total number of pentameters	Short vowel endings	Percentage
Tib. I and II	619	27	4·35
Tib. (Lygd.)	145	13	8
Corp. Tib.	91	4	4·45
Propertius[2]	2002	75	4
Ovid[3]	11010	110	1

Type of vowel

Except for one instance of 'modŏ' (Prop. I. 9. 4) the vowels in question are -ă or -ĕ. The figures are:

	Total	-ă	-ĕ
Tib. I and II	27	5	22
Tib. (Lygd.)	13	6	7
Corp. Tib.	4	3	1
Propertius	74	54	20
Ovid	110	39	71

[1] But 'Maĕotide' (Ov. *P.* III. 2. 59).
[2] No difference is observable between the four books.
[3] Including *H.* XV–XXI which show no disproportion.

Non-disyllabic endings in -ă and -ĕ

(1) in -*ă*.

Tib. I and II: 'magisteria' (I. 4. 84).

Corp. Tib.: 'Sulpicia' (III. 16. 4).

Propertius: 'auxilia' (I. 1. 26), 'folia' (II. 3. 12), 'historia'
(I. 15. 24; II. 1. 16), 'Iliada' (II. 1. 50), 'maria' (II. 18. 38).

Ovid: 'adulteria' (*Tr.* II. 514), 'Italia' (*Tr.* I. 4. 20).

(2) in -*ĕ*.

Tib. I and II: 'capite' (I. 1. 72; II. 1. 8), 'cinere' (II. 6. 34),
'latere' (I. 5. 62; I. 10. 14; II. 1. 66), 'Venere' (I. 10. 66).

Propertius: 'calybe' (I. 16. 30), 'despicere' (I. 14. 24),
'Iliade' (II. 34. 66), 'opere' (I. 14. 2), 'Venere' (I. 14. 16).

Ovid: 'perlegere' (*P.* II. 2. 6).

Types of word

(1) in -*ă*.

(*a*) Feminine singular and neuter plural possessive pronouns.
Of these there are about twenty in Propertius and about
a dozen in Ovid.

(*b*) Feminine singular substantives such as 'coma', 'via',
'aqua', 'toga', 'historia'.

(*c*) Neuter plural substantives such as 'vada', 'iuga', 'freta',
'fora', 'maria'.

(*d*) Very occasionally neuter plural past participles such as
'rata' (Ov. *H.* XX. 240).

(*e*) The Greek accusative 'Iliada'.

(2) in -*ĕ*.

(*a*) Ablatives such as 'grege', 'ave', 'capite', etc. These are
relatively common; Ovid has 'ope' at the end of the pentameter over twenty times.

(*b*) Imperatives like 'fuge', 'sine', 'date'.

(*c*) The infinitives 'dare', 'fore', 'despicere'.

(*d*) The substantive 'mare'.

In view of the scarcity of words of the type (◡) ă, (◡) ĕ, and (◡) ŏ, it would be rash to generalize; but it certainly looks as though Ovid at least avoided ending his pentameters with -ă where he reasonably could.

(*d*) SYNIZESIS, SYNCOPE, AND VOCALIC DIAERESIS

1. *Syni̧zesis*

By synizesis is meant the fusion of two syllables into one by the coalescence of two adjacent vowels (or of a vowel and a diphthong), e.g. 'dĕīnde' to 'dēīnde'.

Where the first of the contiguous vowels is *i* it does not always form a vocalic crasis with the following vowel but rather is consonantalized into a *y* or *j*. The result of this is to lengthen any preceding vowel (if followed by a consonant) by the consequent formation of a double consonant, e.g. 'ăbĭēgnus' to 'ābjēgnus'. Sometimes, however, *i* followed by *i* really coalesces, with the result that the preceding vowel is not lengthened, e.g. 'pĕrīïsse' to 'pĕrīsse'. If such a coalescence of -*ii* is preceded not by a consonant but by yet another vowel, all three may join to make one long syllable, e.g. 'trāĭīce' or (?) 'trāīïce' to 'trāīce'.

Instances of synizesis may be classified under four heads:

(*a*) initial compounding prepositions in -ĕ̆,

(*b*) initial ĕō- or ĕā-,

(*c*) final -ĕā, -ĕī, -ĕō from Latin nouns in -*eus* or Greek nouns in -*ēus*,

(*d*) synizesis of *i* (*ia*, *ie*, *ii*, *iu*).

(*a*) *ante-*

antĕācta	*to* antēācta	Ov. *Am.* II. 8. 25.
antĕĕăt	*to* antĕ(e)ăt	Ov. *A.A.* II. 726.
antĕīre	*to* antēīre	Prop. I. 6. 19; II. 3. 41.

de-[1]

dĕĭn	*to* dēīn	Prop. III. 10. 15, etc.
dĕĭnde	*to* dēīnde	*passim.*
dĕhinc	*to* dēīnc	Prop. II. 3. 50: Ov. *F.* VI. 788.

(*b*)

ĕādem	*to* ēādem	Prop. III. 6. 36.
ĕōdem	*to* ēōdem	Prop. II. 8. 26.
ĕōsdem	*to* ēōsdem	Prop. IV. 7. 7–8.

(*c*) -ĕā

aurĕā	*to* aurēā	Ov. *Am.* I. 8. 59.

-ĕī[2]

Promethĕī	*to* Promethēī	Prop. II. 1. 69.
Persĕī	*to* Persēī	Prop. II. 28. 22; II. 30. 4.
Capanĕī	*to* Capanēī	Prop. II. 34. 40.
Phinĕī	*to* Phinēī	Prop. III. 5. 41.
Atrĕī	*to* Atrēī	Ov. *Am.* III. 12. 39.
Cenchrĕīs	*to* Cenchrēīs	Ov. *Tr.* I. 10. 9.
Thesĕī	*to* Thesēī	Ov. *F.* VI. 737.

[1] 'dein', 'deinde', and 'dehinc' are never found in the elegists except with synizesis. Such forms as 'dērit' (='deerit', Prop. IV. 3. 3), 'dērat' (='deerat', Ov. *H.* X. 37), 'dērant' (='deerant', *ib.* XV. 111), 'dēsse' (='deesse', *ib.* XVIII. 136) are universal. According to the *Thesaurus Linguae Latinae* Latin poetry knows the form 'dēest' only in three very doubtful places in Statius's *Thebaid*.

The elegists use the forms 'di' or 'dei', 'dis' or 'deis' to suit their metrical convenience.

PROSODY

-ĕō

Enipĕō	*to* Enipēō	Prop. I. 13. 21.
Promethĕō	*to* Promethēō	Prop. III. 5. 7.
Nerĕō	*to* Nerēō	Prop. III. 7. 67.
alvĕō	*to* alvēō	Ov. *Am.* II. 13. 9; *F.* v. 637.
Orphĕō	*to* Orphēō	Ov. *Am.* III. 9. 21.
aurĕō	*to* aurēō	Ov. *H.* VI. 49.
Persĕō	*to* Persēō	Ov. *H.* XV. 35.
Thesĕō	*to* Thesēō	Ov. *A.A.* III. 457.

(d) -ia-

sēmĭădaperta	*to* sēmjădaperta	Ov. *Am.* I. 6. 4.
sēmĭănimi(s)	*to* sēmjănimi(s)	Ov. *H.* X. 32; *Tr.* I. 3. 92; *F.* II. 838.

-ie-

ăbĭēgnae[1]	*to* ābjēgnae	Prop. III. 19. 12.
ăbĭēgni	*to* ābjēgni	Prop. IV. 1. 42.

-ii-[2]

rĕdĭisse	*to* rĕdīsse	Prop. IV. 3. 70.
pĕrĭisse	*to* pĕrīsse	Ov. *Am.* II. 2. 10; II. 19. 56; *P.* III. 7. 24.
trāĭĭcĕ	*to* trāīcĕ	Prop. II. 12. 18.[3]
Gābĭī	*to* Gābī[4]	Prop. IV. 1. 34.

[1] But (presumably) '...pulsas ăbĭēgno nosceret arces' (Prop. III. 1. 25).

[2] 'audibat' (Ov. *F.* III. 507) and 'feribant' (*F.* IV. 795) are not 'synizesized' forms of 'audiebat' and 'feriebat', but archaisms; see Kühner, *op. cit.* I, p. 724.

[3] So Phillimore, who reads 'trāīcĕ puella', and so edd. who read 'duella' (i.e. 'trāīcĕ duella'; Butler and Barber, however, give 'trāĭcĕ bella'). Similarly we get 'īnĭcĕ' (i.e. 'īnjĭce') at Ov. *H.* VIII. 16 and 'rēĭcĕ' (i.e. 'rējĭce') at Ov. *Am.* I. 4. 34; *A.A.* I. 695. But see 'rēĭcĕ' (Virg. *Ecl.* III. 96).

[4] E. Bednara, *De sermone dactylicorum latinorum quaestiones* (Vratislava Diss., 1905), p. 28, deals with this usage. He adds 'gratiis' to 'gratis', and remarks on the metrically necessary third declension genitive in *-um* (for *-ium*) as exemplified by 'amant(i)um' (Ov. *Am.* III. 10. 15, etc.), 'nocent(i)um'

-*iu*-

sēmǐūstam   *to* sēmjūstam   Ov. *F.* IV. 167.

2. *Syncope*

By syncope is meant the contraction of a word due to the loss of a medial letter.

(*a*) Where this letter is a vowel the word is shortened by a syllable but no further change occurs. Vowels which admit of syncope are *e*, *i*, and *u*.

e. The elegists write 'dextera' and 'dextra' as suits the metre. Ovid has 'calfacienda'[1] (for 'calefacienda') at *A.A.* II. 214, 'incalfacit' at *F.* IV. 919, 'calfacit' at *F.* IV. 698, and 'recalface' at *A.A.* II. 445.

i. Propertius has 'consumps(s)ti' (for 'consumpsisti') at I. 3. 37, 'duxti' (for 'duxisti', *nisi leg.* duxit) at I. 3. 27, and 'imposta' (for 'imposita') at IV. 2. 29.

u. 'periclum'—'periculum', 'saeclum'—'saeculum', 'spectaclum'—'spectaculum' and 'vinclum'—'vinculum' are used as metre demands.

(*b*) Where the lost letter is a consonant or semi-consonant hiatus is caused and, as a rule, synizesis follows. This happens with medial *h*, *m*, *s*, and *v*.

h. Propertius has 'mi' for 'mi(h)i' (I. 12. 19; II. 18. 30; II. 22. 1, etc.), though neither Tibullus nor Ovid uses

(Ov. *P.* I. 8. 19), 'vigil(i)um' (Ov. *Am.* I. 9. 27). Such dative forms as 'casu' (Ov. *A.A.* III. 155), cited by Bednara—to which he might have added 'manu' (Prop. I, II. 12; and (?) II. I. 66, IV. 6. 22) and (?) 'tumultu' (Prop. II. 27. 7) —are archaic and have nothing to do with synizesis.

'Gabi' is nominative plural. *Genitives* in -(*i*)*i*, e.g. 'sacrifici' (nom. 'sacri- ficium'; Ov. *P.* III. 2. 57), do not concern us, as -*i* (not -*ii*) was, at the time at which the elegists wrote, the normal genitive form of -*io* stems (Stolz- Schmalz[5], p. 268), though the poets adopted the form -*ii* if it suited their metrical convenience.

[1] Quintilian (I. 6. 21) suggests that 'calfacere' was the usual pronunciation.

the short form. 'nil'[1] for 'ni(h)il' is common in all the elegists.

m. This letter drops out in certain verbal compounds of *circum.* Synizesis does not occur. Instances are: 'circŭĭere' (Prop. II. 5. 26), 'circŭĭt' (Ov. *Am.* III. 2. 69), 'circŭĕunda' (Ov. *A.A.* III. 396), and 'circŭĕuntis' (Ov. *P.* I. 2. 20).

s. Tibullus (I. 4. 63) writes 'ni' for 'ni(s)i', and Ovid does the same several times (e.g. *H.* VIII. 102). Propertius does not use 'ni'.

v. Ovid has 'flesti' for 'fle(v)isti' (*H.* V. 43, 45), 'flesset' for 'fle(v)isset' (*R.A.* 606), 'scisse' for 'sci(v)isse' (*F.* VI. 336). Opinion is divided as to 'flemus' (Prop. II. 7. 2) and 'narramus' (*ib.* 15. 3). These may stand for, respectively, 'fle(v)imus' and 'narra(v)imus' or be present (not perfect) indicatives. Forms such as 'negarat' for 'nega(v)erat' (e.g. Prop. II. 22. 11) are not uncommon.[2] In one case the hiatus, consequent upon the loss of *v,* stands: 'scĭĕro' for 'scīvĕro' (Ov. *H.* XIX. 117).

3. *Vocalic diaeresis*

By this is meant the splitting of one syllable into two by the vocalizing of a consonant, e.g. 'volŭĭt' from 'volvĭt'. Instances of this are rare and mostly confined to the verbs 'solvo' ('soluo') and 'volvo' ('voluo') and their compounds. When these verbs are found at certain positions in the line it is impossible to tell whether the vocalic or the consonantal form of *u* (*v*) is intended. The following words, for example, may be scanned as choriambs or molossi:

exsŏlŭit (exsŏlvit) promissa Venus	*Corp. Tib.* III. 13. 5.
vota ego persŏlŭam (persŏlvam)	Ov. *H.* VI. 75.

[1] Housman, *C.R.* XXXIII (1919), pp. 56 sqq., shows that Ovid always uses 'nihil' (not 'nil') in the arsis of the first foot.

[2] For a full list see Bednara, *op. cit.* p. 39.

But in other cases the nature of u (v) is clear from the metre, e.g.

persolvit vota procellis	Prop. II. 25. 23.
votum persolvit, at illi	Prop. II. 26. 49.
involvit, et ignes	Ov. *F.* IV. 705.

What makes diaeresis certain is the appearance of the word in the second half of the pentameter. Such cases are:

dissŏlŭenda	Tib. I. 7. 2	dissŏlŭantur[1]	Ov. *Tr.* IV. 8. 18
dissŏlŭisse	Tib. I. 10. 62	exsŏlŭisse	Ov. *F.* IV. 534
sŏlŭisse	*Corp. Tib.* III.	persŏlŭere	Ov. *F.* V. 330
	II. 16	invŏlŭisse	Ov. *H.* IX. 86
persŏlŭenda	Ov. *H.* VI. 74	evŏlŭisse	Ov. *H.* XII. 4

'mīlŭus'[2] seems to be the normal scansion: Ov. *Am.* II. 6. 34; *F.* III. 794, 808.

The perfect of *consuesco*[3] appears in two forms:

qui iam consūēvi fortiter esse miser   Ov. *Tr.* V. 11. 4.

but

aptaque consueras accipere, apta dare   Ov. *H.* XV. 130.

where the scansion is presumably 'consŭĕras' (though it might be 'consūēras').

---

[1] If this be the right reading.

[2] 'milvi' occurs at the end of a line (94) in the *Halieuticon*.

[3] Propertius has 'nos, ut consuemus, nostros agitamus amores' (I. 7. 5); on which Butler and Barber remark 'perhaps a contraction for "consuevimus" ...but "sueo" existed'.

(e) ELISION[1]

An examination of 200 lines of Catullus's elegiacs, taken at random, shows the following elisions: short open vowels, 39; -m, 32; long open vowels, 32; diphthongs, one; total, 104.

The figures for a similar number of lines so taken from the three elegists are:[2]

	◡	-m	–	Diphthongs	Total	Percentage
Tibullus	20	5	3	–	28	14
Prop.[3] I	25	10	3	–	38	19
Prop. IV	28	12	6	–	46	23
Ov. *A.A.* II	17	2	3	–	22	11
Ov. *Tr.* II	21	2	3	–	26	13

[1] The subject is treated by A. Siedow, *De elisionis aphaeresis hiatus usu in hexametro latino ab Ennii usque ad Ovidii tempora* (Greifsw. Diss., 1911).

[2] The figures here given were arrived at independently but tally almost exactly with those given by R. G. Kent (*Trans. Am. Phil. Ass.* LIV, 1923, pp. 68–97). According to Kent, Tib. I and II has fifteen elisions per hundred lines, whilst Ovid, who varies between 10% and 16%, shows a general average of 13%; Propertius is not considered in his article.

In an earlier paper, 'Elision and hiatus in Latin prose and verse' (*Trans. Am. Phil. Ass.* XLVI, 1915), the same scholar and E. H. Sturtevant give (pp. 148–50) the following figures: Tib. I, thirteen elisions per hundred lines; Prop. I–II. 9, 22; Ov. *Am.* I and II, nine; and Ov. *Tr.* I and II, fourteen. Both articles deal also with the various types of elision, dividing them into elisions of (1) short vowels (other than -*que*), (2) long vowels, (3) -*que* (together with such words as *quisque*, etc.), (4) -*m*, (5) prodelision of *est*. The later article gives the following percentages: Of the total number of elisions in Tib. I and II 39% are of type (1), 26% of type (5), 13% of type (3), 13% of type (4), and 9% of type (2). Of the total number of elisions in Ovid, 38% are of type (5), 26% of type (1), 23% of type (3), 7% of type (4), and 6% of type (2).

In the earlier article the following relative frequencies are given:

	◡	–	'*st*	-*m*	-*que*
Tib. I (106 elisions)	38	9	30	12	11
Prop. I–II. 9 (228 elisions)	41	7	12	25	15
Ov. *Am.* I and II (211 elisions)	30	8	37	10	15
Ov. *Tr.* I and II (183 elisions)	24	3	43	6	24

[3] Hosius in his third edition (1932) gives (p. 180) the total number of elisions in the four books as 909. This average (22%) tallies almost exactly with my figures for bks I and IV: 38+46 in 200 lines=21%.

Thus while Catullus has rather more than one elision in every couplet, Ovid, in his earlier poetry, allows himself only a little more than one in every five.

Types of elision

Even more remarkable than the smaller *total number* of elisions in the later elegists as compared with Catullus is the smaller number in their verses of elisions of long vowels and *-m* endings.

Elision of short vowels requires no comment,[1] except that such elision at the end of dactylic words before a short initial vowel, though quite legitimate, is rare, e.g. 'noxĭ(ă) Ālexandria' (Prop. III. 11. 33).

Elision of *-m*, though commoner before initial long vowels, is freely used before short ones, e.g. 'scrib(am) ĭgitur' (Prop. II. 5. 27). Cretics in *-m* are not elided before an initial short vowel except for 'huic ego, vae, demens narrabam flūmĭn(um) ămores' (Ov. *Am.* III. 6. 101)—a unique instance.[2] The same holds good for cretics ending in a long vowel. Of this no instance is found.[3]

---

[1] H. Mirgel, *De synaloephis et caesuris in versu hexametri latini* (Gottingen Diss., 1910), citing Luetjohann (*Commentationes Propertianae*, Kiel, 1869, p. 103), gives (p. 17) the total number of elisions in Propertius as 1005 (see note 3, p. 72) of which 555 take the form (◡) −, 333 (◡) ◡, 91 (−) −, and 26 (−) ◡; from which we see that even in the poet least careful about elision the proportion of elided short to elided long syllables is almost eight to one. In the 772 lines of Ov. *A.A.* I the figures are: 21 (◡) −, 44 (◡) ◡, three (−) −, and six (-*m*)- which may be classed as (◡) −; none of (−) ◡. Here the proportion of elided short to elided long vowels, therefore, is about 24 to 1.

[2] He has 'virgin(em) et unam' at *Met.* VI. 524.

[3] As has already been said (see p. 58) 'Castŏr(i) Amyclaeo...' (Ov. *H.* VIII. 71) is certainly spurious, and even if it were not the *i* might be regarded as Greek and so short. Final *i* (except for 'mihĭ', 'tibĭ', and 'sibĭ') is very rare in Latin. Ovid elides one at *A.A.* III. 672: 'Lemnias(ĭ) et gladios.'

Elision of final long vowels falls under two heads:

A. *Before initial short vowels*

Of this there are eleven types:

(1) -(*ē*) *ă*-. Rare, and confined to monosyllables: 't(ē) ălii' (Prop. II. 11. 1); 'm(ē) ăb amore' (Prop. II. 25. 9); 'm(ē) ăliquid' (Ov. *Tr.* v. 10. 41).

(2) -(*ē*) *ĕ*-. Rare: 'quar(ē) ĕgo' (Tib. (Lygd.) III. 4. 49); 't(ē) ĕgo' (Prop. II. 20. 11; Ov. *Am.* II. 10. 3). Ovid, however, writes 'cert(ē) ĕgo' some dozen times.

(3) -(*ī*) *ă*-. Very rare; perhaps only 'nov(ī) ăliquam' (Ov. *Am.* II. 17. 29); 'sumps(ī) ănimum' (Ov. *F.* I. 147).

(4) -(*ī*) *ĕ*-. Most of the instances take the form of the first person singular of the perfect indicative followed by *ego*. Tibullus has 'vid(ī) ĕgo' once, Propertius five times, and Ovid eleven. Other perfects so elided (all in Propertius) are *odi, dixi, sensi,* and *respondi*—all followed by *ego*. Further, Tibullus writes 'ill(ī) ĕtiam' (II. 1. 41) and Ovid 'vid(ī) ĕtiam' (*H.* XII. 91).

(5) -(*ō*) *ă*-. There are eight cases in Ovid of *ergo* before -*ă*, but the *o* of *ergo* is of doubtful quantity (see p. 52). Otherwise perhaps only 'aequ(ō) ănimo' (Ov. *Am.* II. 7. 12), probably helped by the existence of the adjective *aequanimus*.

(6) -(*ō*) -*ĕ*. 'erg(ō) ĕgo' (Prop. III. 21. 17), and a dozen times in Ovid, who also elides this *ŏ* before *etiam, erat, erit,* and *eat*. Ovid has 'quand(ō) ĕgo' three times and 'quand(ō) ĕrit' twice; but the *o* of *quando*, though long in the elegists (see above, p. 53), was short in later Latin.

So, again, Propertius elides the *o* of *credo, flebo, iuro,* and *celo* before *ego*, and Ovid once writes 'cred(ō) ĕtiam' (*Am.* III. 7. 45); but, as has been said (see above, p. 51), the final *o* of verbs tended to be *anceps*. The only two unequivocal cases are: 'In(ō) ĕtiam' (Prop. II. 28. 19); 'Bacch(ō) ĕt Apolline' (Prop. III. 2. 9).

(7) -(ō) ĭ-. Very rare; perhaps only 'imm(ō) ĭta' (Ov. *Tr.* I. 2. 99; III. 14. 7).

(8) -(ō) (h)ŏ-. Very rare; perhaps only 'erg(ŏ) hŏminum' (Ov. *Tr.* II. 87).

(9) -(ō) ŭ-. 'erg(ŏ) ŭbi' occurs seven times in Ovid.

(10) -(ū) ă-. Perhaps only 't(ū) ăliud' (Ov. *F.* VI. 291).

(11) -(ū) ĕ-. Perhaps only 't(ū) ĕtiam' (Prop. II. 18. 19).

B. *Before initial long vowels*[1]

Elisions of long open vowels or diphthongs before initial vowels long by quantity or position or before diphthongs form a more numerous and a more diversified class. There are 31 types:

(1) -(ā) ā-.[2] 'invidi(ā) admirante' (Prop.[3] II. 17. 11): 'long(ā) adsuetudine' (Ov. *Tr.* I. 6. 27); 'aus(ā) atque ausura' (III. 9. 16).

(2) -(ā) ē-. 'concelebr(ā) et multo' (Tib. I. 7. 50): 'supposit(ā) excipiens' (Prop. II. 32. 40): 'form(ā) et meritis' (Ov. *H.* XV. 188).

(3) -(ā) ī-. 'oper(ā) insuetas' (Tib. I. 4. 48); 'frustr(ā) immeritum' (Tib. (Lygd.) III. 4. 14): 'su(ā) in muri' (Prop. III. 2. 6).

(4) -(ā) ō-. 'qu(ā) Ortygiae' (Prop. III. 22. 15): 'contr(ā) obicies' (Ov. *Am.* II. 2. 37).

(5) -(ā) ae-. 'ill(ā) aetate' (Prop. IV. 1. 127).

[1] Apparent elisions before *est* and (rarely) *es* are really prodelisions of the *e* of those words; whence the practice of some editors of printing, e.g., 'meost' for 'meo (e)st'. In what follows this prodelision is ignored.

[2] Quintilian (IX. 4. 33) comments on the viciousness of the elision between *similar* long vowels: 'pessime longae, quae easdem inter se literas committunt, sonabunt.'

[3] And 'qu(ā) alludit', if Lambinus's 'alludit' for the MSS. 'ludit' at III. 18. 1 be accepted.

(6) -(ĕ) ā-. About nine instances occur in the elegists, in all of which the elided vowel is that of *me*, *te*, or *se*.

(7) -(ĕ) ē-. A dozen instances in which *me*, *te*, or *se* is elided; otherwise only 'faci(ē) et regalibus' (Prop. IV. 4. 21): 'sollicit(ē) expectas' (Ov. *A.A.* III. 749).

(8) -(ĕ) ī-. Twenty cases of the elision of the *e* of the accusative or ablative of the personal pronouns; otherwise perhaps only 'cert(ē) isdem' (Prop. II. 26. 43): 'tim(ē) insidias' (Ov. *Am.* II. 19. 20); 'moderat(ē) iniuria' (*A.A.* III. 683); 'cert(ē) in patria' (*Tr.* IV. 2. 64).

(9) -(ĕ) ō-. Perhaps only 's(ē) odisse' (Prop. II. 26. 25).

(10) -(ĕ) ū-. Six cases in all, and all these the elision of the *e* of *me*, *te*, and *se*.

(11) -(ĕ) au-. 'm(ē) audacius' (*Corp. Tib.* III. 19. 19).

(12)[1] -(ĕ) eu-. 's(ē) Europen' (Ov. *A.A.* I. 323).

(13) -(ĭ) ā-. 'cupid(ī) ad ripas' (Tib. II. 5. 54). There are nine instances in Propertius, two of them monosyllabic: 's(ī) altera' (II. 14. 10); 'qu(ī) ad vadimonia' (IV. 2. 57). Ovid has 'ill(ī) a caelo' (*F.* VI. 32).

(14) -(ĭ) ē-. One Tibullan and five Ovidian instances; of Propertius's seven cases three involve *s(ī)*.

(15) -(ĭ) ī-. 's(ī) in molli' (Tib. I. 2. 56); 'flauist(ī) ignoto' (Tib. (Lygd.) III. 6. 40): 'docuist(ī) impune' (Prop. II. 6. 21); 'consimil(i) impositum' (III. 6. 39). Ovid has eight instances.

(16) -(ĭ) ō-. 'qu(ī) officia' (Prop. II. 25. 39): 'vid(ī), obstipui' (Ov. *H.* XVI. 135); 'fugient(i) obsistite' (*F.* II. 595—a unique line, as it also contains 'ill(ī) in prima').

(17) -(ĭ) ū-. 'tant(ī), ut tantus' (Ov. *H.* IX. 10); 'nasc(ī) ut posses' (*P.* I. 2. 3).

(18) -(ĭ) ae-. Perhaps only 'qu(ī) aestivos' (Prop. III. 20. 11).

---

[1] In (6) to (12) inclusive the comparative frequency of *m(e)*, *t(e)*, and *s(e)* is remarkable.

(19) -(ī) *au*-. 'rem(ī) aut' (Prop. II. 1. 23): 'vid(ī) aut' (Ov. *H*. X. 31).

(20) -(ō) *ā*-. Not (relatively speaking) uncommon; over a dozen cases in all, two of the Ovidian ones being *erg(ŏ)*.

(21) -(ō) *ē*-. Ten cases; none is *erg(ŏ)*.

(22) -(ō) *ī*-. Propertius has three cases; Ovid five, three of which are *erg(ŏ)*.

(23) -(ō) *ō*-. Rare. 'Mercuri(o) Ossaeis' (Prop. II. 2. 11; if Burmann's correction be accepted); 'virg(ō), officiis' (IV. 4. 92): 'erg(ŏ) omnis' (Ov. *Tr*. IV. 2. 19).

(24) -(ō) *ū*-. 'ade(ō) ut noceat' (Prop. III. 16. 14): 'facit(ō), ut dicas' (Ov. *H*. XIII. 69), and five cases of *erg(ŏ)*.

(25) -(ō) *ae*-. Perhaps only 'mors(ō) aequales' (Prop. III. 8. 21).

(26) -(ō) *au*-. 'quaerend(ō) audita' (Prop. II. 22. 49); 'vol(ō) aut' (III. 8. 23): 'erg(ŏ) aut' (Ov. *A.A*. II. 285); 'lin(ō) aut' (*R.A*. 208); 'Tithon(ō) Aurora' (*F*. I. 461).

(27) -(ae) *ā*-. 'qu(ae) abducis' (Tib. II. 3. 61); 'praefat(ae) ante' (III. 2. 15); 'Europ(ae) atque' (Prop. II. 3. 36); 'mult(ae) ante' (III. 20. 19): 'cult(ae) accedere' (Ov. *Am*. II. 4. 37); 'decept(ae), a!' (*A.A*. III. 454); 'doct(ae) assensere' (*F*. VI. 811).

(28) -(ae) *ē*-. 'aeri(ae) et nubes' (Tib. (Lygd.) III. 6. 28: 'Id(ae) et cupido' (Prop. I. 2. 17); 'vit(ae) et morti' (II. 1. 74); 'Ortygi(ae) et visenda' (III. 22. 15; see (4)).

(29) -(ae) *ī*-. 'demiss(ae) in pocula' (Prop. II. 33. 37); 'Helen(ae) in gremio' (III. 8. 32); 'timid(ae) inclamasse' (Ov. *Am*. I. 7. 45); 'decept(ae) ignoscere' (*P*. IV. 6. 15).

(30) -(ae) *ū*-. Perhaps only 'ver(ae) ut lateant' (Ov. *Am*. II. 2. 31).

(31) -(ae) *au*-. Perhaps only 'furi(ae) aut' (Prop. III. 5. 41). As may be seen in some of the above cited instances, to which may be added 'fidus er(ō): in nostros curre, puella, toros'

(Prop. III. 20. 10), elision may take place over a mark of punctuation.

Monosyllabic elision

Mention has already been made of the not infrequent elision of *me*, *te*, and *se*. Of the total number of monosyllabic elisions in the elegists these words form more than 50%. Other monosyllables susceptible to elision are: *cum* (conjunction; *cum* preposition is never elided), *dem*,[1] *iam*, *qua* (='where'), *qui* and *quae* (relatives), *si*, *sim*, *sum*, *tam*, *tum*.

Monosyllabic elision occurs usually before a long initial vowel, but (besides 't(ē) ĕgo' noticed above) *cum*, *iam*, *sum*, and *tum* are all occasionally found elided before a short one. Instances are: 's(um) ego' (Prop. I. 12. 11: Ov. *Am.* II. 8. 13; *Tr.* III. 11. 25); 't(um) ego' (Prop. II. 26. 9); 'c(um) ita' (Ov. *Am.* I. 5. 15); 'i(am) abiere' (Prop. II. 16. 33).

Figures for monosyllabic elision are:

	Elision of *me*, *te*, *se*	Other monosyllables	Total
Tibullus	7	3	10
Propertius	19	29	48
Ovid	23	12	35
Total	49	44	93

Elision of 'atque'[2]

It may be of interest to test the validity of the old rule which forbade the use of unelided *atque* in elegiacs in the light of

[1] A solitary instance in Ov. *A.A.* III. 2.

[2] B. Axelson, *Unpoëtische Wörter* (Lund, 1945), pp. 83–4, notes the reluctance of the poets of the golden age (with the exception of Horace) to use unelided *atque*. He observes, *inter alia*, that of the 35 instances of unelided *atque* (as against 294 of elided) in the *Aeneid*, 27 occur in bks VII–XII. For a fuller treatment of this question see *C.Q.* XLII (1948), pp. 91–3. I may perhaps be allowed here to quote the final paragraph of my article: 'These are the facts. When we ask *why* they are so, we are on less sure ground.

the actual practice of the elegiac writers themselves. There are in all nineteen instances, or possible instances, where unelided *atque* is found: three in Tib. I and II, one in Tib. (Lygd.), three in Propertius, and twelve in Ovid. Of these nineteen cases four are at least suspect for other reasons. These are:

atque tubas atque arma ferunt   Tib. II. 5. 73.

Except perhaps for 'atque deos atque astra vocat' (Virg. *Ecl.* v. 23),[1] this use of the double *atque* is unknown in Latin poetry until the time of Silius Italicus.[2]

corniger atque dei   Prop. III. 13. 39.

This, the MSS. reading, is kept by Phillimore; but Butler and Barber accept Hertzberg's 'corniger Arcadii'.

atque vades sponsum stultos   Ov. *Am.* I. 13. 19.

So Ehwald; there is MSS. confusion here, and Withof's 'atqu(e) eadem sponsum multos' is at least as likely as Ehwald's reading.

sufficit atque malis   Ov. *Tr.* III. 2. 13.

So the Laurentian MS. (kept by Ehwald-Levy); but as Owen's Γ (i.e. the consensus of the five next best MSS.) gives 'suffecit-

The only reason that suggests itself is something like this: *atque*, which despite its five letters is of no more semantic use than the three-letter *-que* and of less than the two-letter *et*, may have been felt by at any rate careful Latin poets to arrogate to itself more room than it was really worth. By means of elision they could (and so did) reduce the word to a size more in keeping with its semantic value.'

[1] Stolz-Schmalz[5] (*op. cit.* p. 663) and the *Thesaurus* both doubt this case; for if, with Ribbeck, one understands 'est' with 'complexa' in l. 22 and puts a comma at the end of that line, then the first 'atque' joins the verbs 'complexa (est)' and 'vocat' while the second merely connects 'deos' with 'astra'. It should perhaps be added (though it is ignored by Stolz-Schmalz) that at Virg. *Georg.* IV. 463 we find 'atque Getae atque Hebrus'.

[2] Sil. I. 93.

que', it seems better to accept this (as Merkel does) rather than saddle Ovid with postponed and unelided 'atque'.

Eleven more cases offer variant readings or admit of simple emendation. These are:

> atque tua labens navita fleret aqua   Prop. II. 26. 8.

It is of course easy to understand 'te' as the object of 'fleret', but 'teque' for 'atque' would not be a bold emendation.

> te canit atque suum pubes miratur Osirim
> barbara   Tib. I. 7. 27–8.

The meaning is 'sing of you [Nile], and admire you as they admire their god, Osiris' and Tibullus may well have written 'utque'.[1]

> atque morer, me, me sustineamque, rogat   Ov. *A.A.* II. 690.

Some MSS. apparently read 'utque'; and certainly 'rogat ut morer' is as good Latin as 'rogat morer'.

> atque sit in nobis pars bona salva facis   Ov. *P.* III. 2. 4.

Here again some MSS. give 'utque'; and again 'facis ut bona sit' is no worse Latin than 'facis bona sit'.

> atque suis numeris forte quievit opus   Ov. *P.* II. 9. 60.

Here the *codd. dett.* give 'utque'; and, with *ut* meaning 'when', this may be right. Perhaps, however, a more likely reading is 'aque'.[2] With *quiescere* in the sense of 'rest from' the *a* is almost necessary:[3] cf. 'requiescens a reipublicae...

---

[1] Postgate, in his Loeb translation, gives 'thou art sung and worshipped *as* their own Osiris'. (I have a suspicion that 'utque' has been proposed here, but cannot trace the reference.)

[2] For *aque* see 'aque domo' (Ov. *P.* I. 8. 33); 'aque tuis' (*ib.* 9. 48). See also 'aque tua est nostra spreta parente parens?' (Ov. *H.* XXI. 180), where all editors accept Bersmann's 'aque' for MSS. 'atque'.

[3] Kühner, *op. cit.* II. i, p. 493.

muneribus' (Cic. *de Off.* III. 2); 'requiesse auris a strepitu'
(Livy XXVI. 22. 8), etc.

atque sua caesum matre queruntur Ityn   Ov. *Am.* II. 14. 30.

Here 'aque' would give us the more normal 'caesum a matre'
for the (certainly possible) 'caesum matre'.

atque procul Latio diversum missus in orbem

Ov. *Tr.* IV. 2. 69.

procul with the bare ablative is of course correct (e.g. Ov. *P.*
I. 5. 73), but it is much commoner with *a*; should we read
here 'aque'?[1]

atque mea terra prope sunt funebria saxa   Ov. *Tr.* IV. 4. 85.

Owen in his 1889 edition conjectured 'aque', which has been
justified by the Trèves MS., and 'aque' now appears in his
Oxford Classical Text and in Ehwald-Levy.

me . . . Charybdis

devoret atque suis ad Styga mittat aquis   Ov. *Tr.* V. 2. 73–4.

Here Heinsius conjectured 'aque'.

atque meis distent ut tua fata, vale   Ov. *Tr.* V. 13. 34.

Here again 'aque' would give a slightly more usual construction.

constitit, atque caput niveo velatus amictu   Ov. *F.* III. 363.

Though the grammar of this is unimpeachable, Ovid *may*
have written 'aque', for he had a marked penchant for using
a and *ab* with instrumental ablatives. There are some twenty
instances of this in his poems.[2]

The only four cases which defy easy emendation on these
lines are:

atque satur libo sit madeatque mero   Tib. II. 2. 8.

[1] For the tmesis 'a . . . Latio' see p. 99.
[2] See Owen on *Tr.* II. 28.

ille ego Latonae filius atque Iovis   Tib. (Lygd.) III. 4. 72.

tempore quo sociis venit Lycomedius armis
    atque Sabina feri contudit arma Tati   Prop. IV. 2. 51–2.

decidit, atque cadens 'pater, o pater, auferor' inquit[1]
                                 Ov. *A.A.* II. 91.

Place of elision

A. IN THE HEXAMETER

Elisions are found at every caesura, strong and weak, and every diaeresis of the line. There are thus sixteen types, e.g.

(1) at 1 *s*:

    cumqu(e) ⋮ ego deficiam, nec possum ducere currum
                               Ov. *P.* III. 1. 67.

(2) at 1 *w*:

    me quoqu(e) ⋮ amicorum nimio terrore metuque
                               Ov. *P.* III. 2. 15.

(3) at 1 *d*:

    quos utin(am) | in nobis, vita, experiare labores
                           Prop. II. 24. 29.

(4) at 2 *s*:

    quae si fort(e) ⋮ aliquid vultu mihi dura negarat
                           Prop. II. 22. 11.

(5) at 2 *w*:

    si libitum tib(i) ⋮ erit, Lernaeas pugnet ad hydras
                           Prop. II. 24. 25.

(6) at 2 *d*:

    duritia ferr(um) | ut superes adamantaque teque
                           Ov. *H.* II. 137.

(7) at 3 *s*:

    exerces pretios(a) ⋮ odia et constantia magno   Ov. *H.* VII. 47.

(8) at 3 *w*:

    ter volui promitter(e) ⋮ opem, ter lingua retenta est
                           Ov. *F.* V. 247.

---

[1] Is it possible that Ovid wrote '"a"que cadens "pater, o pater, auferor" inquit'? If he could say '"io"que...canet' (*Tr.* IV. 2. 51), why not '"a" que'?

(9) at 3 d:

omnia, crede mihi, tec(um) | uno munera lecto

Prop. II. 11. 3.

(10) at 4 s:

et quamvis duplici corrept(um) ⦂ ardore iuberent

Prop. I. 3. 13.

(11) at 4 w:

ipse ego segnis eram discinctaqu(e) ⦂ in otia natus

Ov. *Am.* I. 9. 41.

(12) at 4 d:

inter quos Helene nudis caper(e) | arma papillis

Prop. III. 14. 19.

(13) at 5 s:

hoc etiam grave erat, nulla merced(e) ⦂ hyacinthos

Prop. IV. 7. 33.

(14) at 5 w:

donec eras simplex, animum cum corpor(e) ⦂ amavi

Ov. *Am.* I. 10. 13.

(15) at 5 d:

nec refero solisque vias et qualis, ub(i) | orbem   Tib. II. 4. 17.

? (16) at 6 s:

assideant fratres iuxta, Minoia sell(a), ⦂ et   Prop. IV. 11. 21.

Of these (1)–(5), (10) and (12) need no comment, except the obvious one that, by reason of the comparative rarity of words in Latin that begin iambically and end dactylically, elision at weak caesuras is not very common.

(6). Rare; Tibullus has three instances,[1] and Ovid, in all his eleven thousand odd hexameters, only ten.[2] Propertius, however, runs to 21, three of which take the form $-\cup\cup\,|-\cup\,⦂\,\cup(-)\,⦂|-\,⦂$. These are:

regnave prima ⦂ Rem(i) ⦂| aut ⦂ animos Carthaginis altae II. 1. 23.

---

[1] I. 2. 59; II. 3. 59; II. 5. 73.

[2] *H.* II. 137; XIII. 141; *A.A.* I. 487; II. 397; *Tr.* I. 3. 89; IV. 2. 55; *P.* I. 4. 7; II. 6. 23; *F.* III. 585; VI. 443.

tela fugacis ⋮ equ(i) ⋮| et ⋮ bracati militis arcus   III. 4. 17.

sacra diesque ⋮ can(am) ⋮| et ⋮ cognomina prisca locorum

IV. 1. 69.

(7). Elision at the main caesura (strong) is not common. Tib. (Lygd.) has one instance,[1] Propertius six,[2] and Ovid 24.

(8). Elision at the main caesura (weak) is very rare. Propertius supplies no instance, Tibullus one,[3] and Ovid two.[4]

(9). Where there is a strong main caesura (as in the instance quoted above), elision at the third diaeresis is not uncommon. Where the main caesura is weak this type of elision is very rare. An instance is:

sub terris sint iura ⋮ de(um) | et tormenta Gigantum

Prop. III. 5. 39.

The reasons for this rarity are obvious: first, the comparative scarcity of the weak caesura; second, the fact that such an elision must either be followed by a fourth-foot dactyl or (as in the instance quoted) occur in a line with no bucolic diaeresis—otherwise a 'false ending' is caused.[5]

(11). Rare; there seem to be no cases in Tibullus, and Propertius and Ovid furnish, respectively, only two[6] and

[1] III. 1. 17.

[2] I. 14. 23; II. 3. 31; II. 10. 1; II. 21. 9; III. 1. 29; III. 15. 23.

[3] I. 6. 33.   [4] *F.* V. 247; VI. 679.

[5] Cf. p. 8. Owen (on *Tr.* II. 296) remarks: 'Ovid in his elegiacs never allows the elision of the final long syllable of a word forming an iambus.' He would emend both 'saepe tim(ē) insidias...' (*Am.* II. 19. 20) and 'disce me(ō) exemplo...' (*H.* XVII. 97). Palmer (on *H.* XVII. 97) agrees as to the corruption of *Am.* II. 19. 20 and only lets *H.* XVII. 97 stand as having been written 'probably fifty or sixty years later than Ovid'. The elision of a final -*m* of an iambic word is rare in Ovid. See Palmer on *H.* XV. 23. Examples are: 'ipse fer(am) ante tuos...' (*Am.* II. 13. 24); 'sume fid(em) et pharetram' (*H.* XV. 23). Where found this elision is usually before *et*. At 'aut in amore dolere vol(o) aut...' (Prop. III. 8. 23) the final -*o* may be regarded as short, as at II. 10. 9. See above, p. 52. Another Propertian example may be seen at III. 13. 61, 'en(im) Ilia'.

[6] III. 9. 39; III. 21. 11.

84

five.[1] In four out of the five Ovidian cases the elided syllable is -*que*.

(13). Besides the Propertian instance quoted there seems to be only 'ascendo (vires animus dabat) atqu(e) ⋮ ita late' (Ov. *H.* X. 27).

(14). Elision at the weak caesura of the fifth foot is less rare than has sometimes been supposed. Except for the unique case of 'flumin(um) amores' (Ov. *Am.* III. 6. 101; see above, p. 73) only the short open vowels -*ă* and -*ĕ* are here elided, and of these elided -*ĕ* is much the commoner. The commonest type of all is the elision of the final -*ĕ* of third conjugation present infinitives. A table of frequencies and totals is given:

| | Totals | -*ĕ* | | | | |
		Present infinitive	Third declension ablative singular	Plural imperative	Singular imperative	-*que* (and *quoque*)
Tibullus	5	4	1	–	–	–
Propertius	29	21	7	1	–	–
Ovid	41	23	10	2	1	5

| | Totals | -*ă* | |
		Feminine singular	Neuter plural
Tibullus	3	1	2
Propertius	1	1	–
Ovid	5	1	4

(15). Only two real cases, 'ub(i) orbem' (Tib. II. 4. 17), and 'ub(i) audis' (Ov. *F.* V. 197), unless elision of the -*ĕ* of *sine* before the word it governs,[2] and of that of *male* before the word it qualifies,[3] be included.

[1] *Am.* I. 9. 41; *H.* VIII. 73; IX. 39; XII. 63; *Tr.* III. 2. 9.
[2] Ov. *Am.* III. 7. 49; *Tr.* V. 7. 33; *P.* II. 11. 19.
[3] Ov. *Tr.* V. 11. 3.

(16). Elision at the sixth caesura is doubtful. As has already been said,[1] '...Minoia | sell(ă) et' (Prop. IV. 11. 21) is almost certainly corrupt; and '...per te, pri|vigne Cu|pid(o), est' (Ov. *Am.* II. 9. 47) is probably a case of prodelision (see p. 13), in spite of the intervening comma.[2]

There are no hypermetric lines in the elegists.

An examination of all the hexameters in Ov. *A.A.* II and of a similar number (373) taken from Tib. I. 6. 1–II. 5. 114 and Prop. II. 1. 1–II. 21. 12 reveals the following frequencies:

Type	Tibullus	Propertius	Ovid
(1)	12	28	10
(2)	4	4	3
(3)	9	35	7
(4)	–	6	1
(5)	1	–	–
(6)	4	11	1
(7)	–	4	2
(8)	1	–	–
(9)	3	9	1
(10)	7	10	5
(11)	–	1	–
(12)	2	2	2
(13)	–	–	–
(14)	3	7	1
(15)	1	–	–
(16)	–	–	–

B. IN THE PENTAMETER

Of the thirteen theoretically possible places in the pentameter—i.e. at each diaeresis and strong or weak caesura—elision is found at nine only. The four non-existent types are shown schematically:

(1) at 1 *s*:

ips(e) ⋮ eques, ipse pedes, signifer ipse fui Ov. *Am.* II. 12. 14.

[1] See p. 13, n. 1.
[2] Manilius supplies a parallel: 'et tu, tricesima summa, es' (IV. 453).

86

(2) at 1 *w*:

    crescit(e) ⠶ et in titulos surgite recta meos   Ov. *H.* V. 24.

(3) at 1 *d*:

    impless(e) | aetatis fata diurna suae   Ov. *H.* VI. 36.

(4) at 2 *s*:

    nec vigilar(e) ⠶ alio nomine cedat Amor   Prop. I. 9. 28.

    at 2 *w*:

    $- \underline{\smallsmile\smallsmile} \,|\, - \smile (\smile) \vdots \smile \,|\, - \,\|\, - \smile\smile \,|\, - \smile\smile \,|\, \underline{\smile}$

    at 2 *d*:[1]

    $- \underline{\smallsmile\smallsmile} \,|\, - \underline{\smallsmile\smallsmile} (\underline{\smile}) \vdots | - \,\|\, - \smile\smile \,|\, - \smile\smile \,|\, \underline{\smile}$

(5) at halfway point:

    quaerere ⠶ non impun(e) || illa rogata venit   Prop. I. 5. 32.

(6) at 3 *s*:

    clamarunt Satyri 'surg(e) ⠶, age, surge, pater!'

                                 Ov. *A.A.* I. 548.

(7) at 3 *w*:

    cui sua 'non feci' dicer(e) ⠶ amica potest   Ov. *Am.* II. 5. 10.

(8) at 3 *d*:

    incipis, incipiet desiner(e) | esse mea   Ov. *Am.* II. 19. 48.

    at 4 *s*:

    $- \underline{\smallsmile\smallsmile} \,|\, - \underline{\smallsmile\smallsmile} \,|\, - \,\|\, - \smile\smile \,|\, - (\smile) \vdots \smile\smile \,|\, \underline{\smile}$

(9) at 4 *w*:

    hippomanes cupidae stillat ab inguin(e) ⠶ equae

                                  Tib. II. 4. 58.

    at 4 *d*:

    $- \underline{\smallsmile\smallsmile} \,|\, - \underline{\smallsmile\smallsmile} \,|\, - \,\|\, - \smile\smile \,|\, - \smile\smile (\smile) \vdots | \underline{\smile}$

---

[1] 'irascor quoniam es, lente, moratus heri' (Prop. III. 23. 12) is of course a case of prodelision. On the impossibility of this elision see Housman in *C.Q.* XXI (1927), p. 6.

Types (1)–(4) require no comment.

(5). Very rare; besides the example quoted there are only:

post etiam collo s(e) implicuisse volet   Tib. I. 4. 56.
immortalis ero, s(i) altera talis erit   Prop. II. 14. 10.

which are to be regarded rather as elisions of the first syllable of the third foot, and

Herculis Antaeiqu(e), Hesperidumque choros

Prop. III. 22. 10.

(6). There is one case in Tibullus,[1] 25 cases in Propertius,[2] and six in Ovid.[3] -m is seldom elided here and a long open vowel never, except for 'cert(e)' in one of the later *Heroides*.[4] Palmer (on *H*. xv. 96) remarks that Ovid 'never elides the second syllable of the second half of the pentameter, whether that syllable is long, short, or ends in -m'. The truth is that, except in the later *Heroides*, he only elides a short open vowel here, and that very seldom.

(7). The commonest type of elision in the second half of the pentameter. Tibullus[5] shows five cases, Propertius[6] 22, and Ovid[7] 34. There is no case of an elided long vowel or -m.

---

[1] II. 1. 40.

[2] I. 3. 44; 9. 34; *10. 16: II. 3. 50; 9. 36; 14. 18 ('nem(ŏ)'); *24. 40; 26. 28: III. *2. 20; 6. 38; 8. 18; *8. 22; 13. 6; *15. 40; 15. 42; 16. 4; 17. 8; 21. 26; *22. 12; 23. 24: IV. *1. 30; 1. 36 (reading either 'long(e)' or 'long(a)'); *7. 48; 8. 6; *8. 70. (Asterisks denote elision of -m: the rest are elisions of short open vowels.)

[3] *H*. *xv. 96; xx. 178: *A.A.* I. 548: *R.A.* 668: *Tr.* III. 6. 6: *P.* III. 1. 90.

[4] *H*. xx. 178. At Prop. IV. 1. 36 'longa', not 'longe' should be read.

[5] I. 2. 10; II. 3. 32; III. 1. 14; III. 4. 84; III. 16. 2 (all (-ĕ)).

[6] I. 3. 16 (if 'sumer(e) et arma' be correct): II. 1. 18; 8. 2; 9. 38; 9. 42; 12. 10; 16. 40; 17. 2; 19. 24; 20. 16; 25. 6; 31. 2; 34. 6: III. 6. 22; 8. 40; 9. 32; 11. 24; 12. 34; 15. 4; 21. 18: IV. 7. 74; 7. 78. Of these sixteen are (-ĕ) (nine present infinitive; four ablative; two imperative; one 'quoque'), three are (-ă), and three (-ī) (dative of personal pronoun singular).

[7] *Am*. I. 11. 26; 13. 22: II. 5. 10: III. 8. 48: *H*. III. 32; IV. 144; XII. 16; XVI. 96; XVIII. 176; XXI. 56: *A.A.* I. 86; II. 672; III. 520: *R.A.* 700: *Tr.* II. 34; 202; 462: III. 2. 24; 14. 26: V. 9. 12: *P.* I. 5. 36; II. 2. 118; III. 1. 144; III. 3. 74;

(8). The second commonest type of elision in the last half of the pentameter. It does not occur in Tibullus, but Propertius has twelve cases and Ovid 35. In only two (possible) cases does the elided syllable end in *-m*. These are:

> nunc tibi pro tumulo Carpathi(um) omne mare est
>
> Prop. III. 7. 12.
>
> an putat ignotam nequiti(am) esse suam   Ov. *Am.* I. 13. 32.

But the authenticity of this last line is very uncertain.

There is no case of an elision of a long open vowel.

The elision of *-ă* at this place is very rare; Propertius supplies a single instance, 'et mari(a) alta domat' (II. 26. 52), and Ovid none. This should cause us to look with some suspicion on Bentley's suggestion 'pomifer(a) arva rigas' at Ov. *Am.* III. 6. 46.

Again, the vowel most often elided is *-ĕ*. Propertius elides 'sin(e)' three times,[1] a present infinitive twice,[2] a plural imperative twice,[3] 'temer(e)' twice,[4] and an ablative once.[5] None of these occur in bk I. Ovid elides the *-ĕ* of the present infinitive sixteen times,[6] '-que' eleven times,[7] and 'sin(e)' four times.[8]

-ĭ is elided only at 'ub(i)' (Ov. *H.* III. 12) and 'nis(i)' (Ov. *A.A.* II. 40).

III. 6. 42; IV. 15. 20: *F.* III. 440; III. 472; IV. 556; V. 56; V. 286; V. 306; V. 486; VI. 306. Of these 28 are (*-ĕ*) (twelve present infinitive; seven '-que' and 'quoque'; five ablative; two imperative; two 'sine'), two are (*-ă*), and four are (*-ĭ*) (two 'tibi', one 'nisi', one 'ubi').

[1] IV. 1. 6; IV. 5. 58; IV. 8. 40.

[2] II. 32. 50; IV. 11. 24 (if 'corripere ore' be read).

[3] III. 1. 2; III. 4. 10.   [4] II. 20. 36; II. 21. 16.

[5] III. 7. 4.

[6] *Am.* II. 19. 48: *H.* III. 40; IV. 30; XI. 54; XI. 88; XII. 50; XII. 166; XIV. 104; XV. 130: *P.* II. 2. 62; II. 3. 38; II. 8. 74; III. 9. 32; IV. 8. 72: *F.* II. 216; VI. 164.

[7] *H.* XIII. 140: *A.A.* III. 802: *Tr.* I. 8. 22; I. 8. 32; II. 226: *P.* III. 4. 24; III. 4. 26: *F.* II. 582; IV. 442; V. 6; V. 274.

[8] *Am.* III. 13. 10: *A.A.* I. 106: *R.A.* 244; 350.

(9). Very rare. Tibullus has the one instance quoted above; Propertius has

> ad vulgi plausus saepe resister(e) equos   III. 4. 14.

and Ovid[1]

> quadriiugos cernes saepe resister(e) equos   *Tr.* IV. 2. 54.
> ad sata fontanas, nec pudet, adder(e) aquas   *P.* I. 8. 46.

An examination of all the pentameters in Ov. *A.A.* II and of a similar number (373) taken from Tib. I. 6. I–II. 5. 114 and Prop. II. I. I–II. 21. 12 shows the following frequencies:

Type	Tibullus	Propertius	Ovid
(1)	7	15	7
(2)	3	9	5
(3)	24	47	5
(4)	2	2	5
(5)	–	1	–
(6)	1	4	–
(7)	1	9	1
(8)	–	1	1
(9)	1	–	–

[1] 'quis scit an et saevas tigridas insul(a) habet' (*H.* x. 86) is palpably corrupt.

CHAPTER V

Word Order and Idiom

(a) POSTPONEMENT OF ENCLITICS

For purely metrical purposes the elegists were in the habit of postponing *-que*, and more rarely *-ve* and *-ne*, so that, instead of being attached to the first word of the sentence or clause, these enclitics were tacked on to the second, third, or fourth. By far the commonest place in which to find these postponed enclitics is in the second half of the pentameter. Here the most usual type is that in which the postponed enclitic is attached to a quadrisyllable, e.g.

in laqueos auceps deciderat*que* suos   Ov. *R.A.* 502.

Of enclitics following quadrisyllabic *verbs* at this place in the line Tibullus furnishes fourteen examples (all in bks I and II), Propertius one,[1] and Ovid 55; following quadrisyllabic *substantives*, Ovid thirteen;[2] following quadrisyllabic *adjectives*, Tib. (Lygd.) one,[3] Ovid two.[4]

Postponed enclitics follow trisyllables at this place in the line more rarely. Tib. I and II has three cases of such an enclitic following a trisyllabic *verb*,[5] and one following a trisyllabic *adjective*;[6] Ovid attaches a postponed enclitic to a trisyllabic *verb*[7] five times.

---

[1] II. 20. 12. It is noteworthy that Propertius is in general very chary of postponing enclitics.

[2] *Am.* III. 14. 12: *A.A.* I. 332; I. 712: *Tr.* I. 2. 104; IV. 5. 6; V. 10. 40: *Ibis* 576: *P.* I. 4. 54; I. 9. 40; III. 6. 48: *F.* I. 246; I. 672; IV. 200.

[3] III. 3. 4.   [4] *Tr.* II. 532; IV. 1. 40.   [5] I. 3. 56; I. 4. 2; II. 6. 52.

[6] II. 3. 38 (reading 'mors propiorque'; some MSS. give 'morsque propinqua').

[7] *H.* XVIII. 94: *A.A.* III. 676: *Tr.* I. 8. 24; III. 8. 38: *P.* I. 4. 38. 'Non videoque' (*Tr.* IV. 6. 48) is scarcely a case.

Postponed enclitics after disyllables (whether of trochaic or iambic scansion) are rare. There are no cases in Tibullus, and Propertius has only

> ornabat niveas nulla*ne* gemma manus?   III. 6. 12.

Ovid supplies four possible instances.[1]

Of the nine instances of postponed enclitics attached to monosyllables eight[2] occur at the start of the second half of the pentameter, e.g.

> ...crines per*que* Minerva suas   Tib. I. 4. 26.

Only one begins the fourth foot:

> ambulat, ingentis varica fert*que* gradus[3]   Ov. *A.A.* III. 304.

Postponed enclitics are found much more rarely in the hexameter: of this there are two cases in Tib. I and II,[4] two or three in Propertius,[5] and perhaps six in Ovid;[6] and in the first half of the pentameter, perhaps uniquely:

> reccidit in*que* suos mensa supina pedes   Prop. IV. 8. 44.

Cases where the enclitic follows not the preposition but the substantive governed by the preposition, e.g.

> qui bene pro patria cum patria*que* iacent   Ov. *H.* III. 106

have not been included in the above survey. Even in prose the enclitic is attached at least as often as not to the substantive.[7]

---

[1] *F.* II. 604 and III. 418 are clear instances. At *P.* II. 1. 6 'verba dedique' may almost be regarded as one word, and at *H.* II. 70 'et Sinis et tauri mixtaque forma viri' (='et mixta forma tauri virique') is rather a case of misplaced than postponed -*que*.

[2] Tib. I. 4. 26: Prop. II. 32. 14; III. 21. 16: Ov. *A.A.* I. 422; III. 302: *Tr.* I. 8. 2: *F.* III. 130; IV. 610.

[3] Here the postponement is eased by the occurrence of 'fertque' in its natural place in l. 302.   [4] I. 10. 51; II. 4. 27.

[5] III. 16. 5; III. 25. 15; IV. 4. 55 (if we accept *N*'s 'pariam*ne*').

[6] *H.* XXI. 19: *Tr.* II. 167: *Ibis* 451; 567: *F.* II. 177; IV. 745 (?).

[7] Kühner, *op. cit.* II. i, p. 583.

NOTE ON WORDS ENDING IN -*ĔQUE*

The apparent reluctance of the prose-writers to attach -*que* to a word ending in -*ĕ* finds its counterpart in the elegists. But just as Cicero allowed himself occasionally such forms as 'ipseque', 'incolumeque', 'Caesareque', 'constituereque', and the like, so in the elegists we find:

redderequ(e)	Tib. I. 3. 34	saepeque	Tib. I. 8. 10
ipseque	*ib.* 5. 11	taleque	Prop. II. 14. 26
sanguinequ(e)	*ib.* 6. 48	iungitequ(e)	Prop. III. 21. 13

Ovid avoids this use altogether, though his ear did not rebel against sounds which seem cacophonous to modern taste, such as:

antiquaque	*Tr.* IV. 1. 87	aequoraqu(e)	*F.* IV. 289
aequaque	*F.* I. 460	sicque	*F.* IV. 848

(*b*) POSTPONEMENT OF NON-ENCLITIC CONJUNCTIONS

The elegiac poets postpone non-enclitic conjunctions, as they do enclitic, *metri gratia.*[1] This postponement may be divided (perhaps rather illogically) into two classes:

1. Postponement of conjunctions which normally stand first word in the sentence or clause to the second or, in rarer cases, the third or fourth place in the sentence or clause in either the hexameter or the first half of the pentameter, e.g.

serica *nam* taceo vulsi carpenta nepotis   Prop. IV. 8. 23.
conveniens miseris *et* quamquam gloria non est

                                 Ov. *P.* IV. 9. 103.
credo ego *sed* multos non habuisse fidem   Prop. II. 24. 42.

[1] See E. Norden, *P. Vergilius Maro, Aeneis Buch VI*[3] (Leipzig, 1926), pp. 402–4.

	A2	A3	A4	B2	B3	B4	B5
at	Prop. IV. I. 95; IV. 10. 23						
atque	Prop. III. 13. 39; Ov. A.A. III. 282						
aut	Prop. II. 13. 50; III. 18. 28			Tib. II. 5. 112	Ov. P. III. 3. 94		
et	Common in all three elegists	Ov. P. IV. 9. 103			Tib. I. 3. 82; I. 9. 16; II. 5. 66; II. 5. 98 Corp. Tib. III. 10. 26 Ov. A.A. III. 376; H. XVI. 26; Tr. V. 7. 40	Tib. I. 2. 96	Ov. P. I. 4. 20
nam	Tib. II. 4. 12 Tib. (Lygd.) III. 4. 43 Prop. IV. 8. 23 Ov. A.A. I. 702; III. 53; H. XI. 61;[1] P. II. I. 53; IV. II. 9; IV. 15. 25; F. I. 59; IV. 64			Ov. Tr. I. 5. 58			
namque	Prop. IV. I. 57; IV. 7. 3 Ov. H. I. 37; Tr. III. I. 10. 47; P. III. 3. 99;[3] F. I. 129			Prop. II. 21. 12			

[1] Reading 'fratris nam nupta'.

[2] 'conveniens animo genus est tibi, nobile namque | pectus...habes'; where (uniquely) 'namque' stands at the end of the line.

	A2	A3	A4	B2	B3	B4	B5
nec (neque)	Tib. I. 1. 72; I. 4. 62; I. 6. 69; I. 7. 26 Tib. (Lygd.) III. 4. 91; III. 6. 55 Prop. III. 14. 28 Ov. H. XVI. 346; P. III. 3. 42	Prop. IV. 5. 57	Tib. (Lygd.) III. 6. 19 Prop. II. 6. 3		Tib. I. 8. 4 Prop. III. 10. 10; IV. 3. 22. 28; IV. 8. 56 Ov. Am. III. 9. 42; III. 12. 42; H. XVIII. 212; Tr. IV. 2. 62; v. 10. 8; P. III. 3. 104; IV. 14. 34; IV. 14. 40	Prop. IV. 11. 94 Ov. H. XVIII. 6; Tr. III. 13. 24	
neve (neu)				Ov. R.A. 628	Prop. III. 12. 12 Ov. Tr. III. 4. 76		
sed	Tib. I. 7. 46; I. 8. 63; II. 4. 3 Tib. (Lygd.) III. 1. 9 Prop. I. 4. 11 Ovid, sixteen cases[1]	Prop. II. 24. 42 Ov. P. IV. 10. 11		Ov. Tr. IV. 1. 66; F. III. 112; VI. 336	Ov. H. XI. 106; XVII. 184; Tr. III. 12. 54; v. 1. 38; P. IV. 9. 124; F. V. 326	Tib. (Lygd.) III. 5. 28	
sive (seu)			Prop. III. 8. 13[2] (?)			Ov. P. II. 10. 34	
vel	Tib. II. 4. 9	Corp. Tib. III. 19. 11					

[1] Am. II. 8. 2: H. XVI. 189; XXI. 192 (with Palmer's punctuation 'permittitur, ipse | sed...'): A.A. III. 479: Tr. I. 2. 109; II 81; III. 2. 7; III. 7. 40: Ibis 140: P. I. 8. 61; II. 2. 126; III. 1. 125; III. 4. 103; III. 5. 11: F. II. 599; III. 182.

[2] If Lachmann's 'seu' be accepted for MSS. 'se'.

95

According as postponement is to the second, third, or fourth place in the sentence or clause these cases will be referred to as A2, A3, and A4.

2. Postponement of such conjunctions to anything from the second to the fifth place in the sentence or clause, occurring *metri gratia* in the second half of the pentameter, e.g.

vera quidem, veri *sed* graviora fide   Ov. *Tr.* IV. 1. 66.
ante meum tempus cogit *et* esse senem   Ov. *P.* I. 4. 20.

According as postponement is to the second, third, fourth, or fifth place in the sentence or clause these cases will be referred to as B2, B3, B4, and B5.

It will be noticed that in the first of the two examples cited above the conjunction occurs first word in the second half of the pentameter. This is the normal form in class B, and to it there are only four exceptions: pentameters in which, as in the second example cited, the conjunction forms the last short syllable of the third foot. The other three exceptions are:

vincta, coronatus stabit *et* ipse calix   Tib. II. 5. 98.
nec mea sunt, fati verba *sed* ista mei   Ov. *Tr.* V. 1. 38.
an scierit Vestam; scisse *sed* ipse negat   Ov. *F.* VI. 336.

The conjunctions susceptible to postponement are *at, atque, aut, et, nam, namque, nec (neque), neve (neu), sed, sive (seu),* and *vel.* From the table on pp. 94–5 it will be seen that A2 is the commonest type and B3 the next commonest.

The conjunctions *autem, enim, igitur,* which usually come second word in their sentence, as well as *ergo* and *etenim* which usually come first, vary in their position even in prose authors[1] and have therefore not been dealt with here.

[1] Kühner, *op. cit.* II. ii, pp. 133 (*autem, enim, igitur*), 139 (*ergo*), 128 (*etenim*).

(c) TMESIS

The commonest, indeed almost the only, form of tmesis[1] in the elegiac poets is that between 'governing' preposition[2] and 'governed' substantive. In other words the elegists allow themselves, for metrical reasons, to hark back to the original adverbial use of what were later prepositions.

The commonest form this tmesis takes (there are some seventy instances of it in Ovid alone) is the interposition between preposition and substantive of a genitive dependent on the substantive, e.g. 'prae *sermonis* amore' (Ov. *Am.* II. 6. 29). This indeed is—speaking logically and not grammatically—not a true tmesis at all; for the genitive is often no more than an adjective qualifying the substantive. Thus, when Ovid writes 'per *avorum* nomina' (*H.* XI. 17), he might as well, but for metre, have written 'per *avita* nomina'.

This form, *p. g. s.*,[3] is, as has been said, by far the commonest; but all three poets show examples of the order *s. p. g.*, e.g. 'limen ad iratae' (*sc.* puellae) (Tib. II. 1. 74), 'face pro thalami'[4] (Ov. *H.* XXI. 172). Occasionally the preposition follows the substantive, which in turn may be preceded by a qualifying adjective or genitive, e.g. 'Augusti puppim super' (Prop. IV. 6. 29); 'me propter' (*ib.* 7. 25); 'caput ante' (Tib. II. 5. 66); 'sanctas heroïdas inter' (Ov. *Tr.* I. 6. 33).

[1] English scholars usually restrict the use of the word *tmesis* to the splitting of words, e.g. Ennius's notorious 'cere- comminuit -brum' for 'cerebrum comminuit'; but, as (*a*) the combination of preposition and substantive really forms one word, and (*b*) Kühner, *op. cit.* II. ii, p. 592, applies the term *tmesis* to the separation of these, I have felt justified in extending the use.

[2] The 'adjurative' *per*, e.g. '*ossa* tibi iuro *per matris*' (Prop. II. 20. 15) has been intentionally excluded from this survey as tmesis involving it is a common prose usage (Kühner, *op. cit.* II. i, pp. 584–5).

[3] In what follows, *p.*=preposition, *g.*=genitive, *s.*=substantive, *a.*= adjective, *ag.*=adjective qualifying the genitive.

[4] See also Ov. *A.A.* III. 805: *Tr.* I. 9. 11; IV. 7. 13: *P.* II. 9. 2: *F.* III. 733.

Sometimes the form is made more elaborate by the addition of not only an adjective qualifying the governed substantive but also an adjective qualifying the genitive. The combination of these four (or five) words appears in the order:

(1). *p. g. a. s.*, e.g.
ad Euxini deformia litora   Ov. *Tr.* v. 2. 63.

(2). *p. ag. s. g.*, e.g.
in laesi verba mariti   Ov. *A.A.* I. 687.[1]

(3). *p. ag. g. s.*, e.g.
in attonitae virginis ore   Ov. *Tr.* III. 9. 18.[2]

(4). *a. p. g. s.*, e.g.
teneris in virginis annis   Ov. *Tr.* III. 7. 17.[3]

(5). *p. ag. a. s. g.*, e.g.
per urbanae splendida castra togae   Ov. *R.A.* 152.[4]

(6). *p. ag. s. a. g.*, e.g.
ad geminae limina prima foris   Ov. *H.* XII. 150.

Sometimes, though rarely, the preposition is severed from its substantive by an adjectival phrase, with or without a preposition of its own, e.g.

praeter *sine pectore* vocem   Ov. *H.* XXI. 141.
de *tanto dignis consule* rebus   Ov. *P.* IV. 5. 22.

Tmesis proper may be said to occur only where one or more words, having no connexion with the substantival phrase

---

[1] See also Ov. *Am.* I. 6. 44: *Tr.* II. 168; III. 9. 2: *F.* III. 664; IV. 907.
[2] See also Ov. *Tr.* IV. 4. 62: *P.* II. 1. 29: *F.* IV. 294.
[3] See also Ov. *P.* II. 2. 19; IV. 5. 1.
[4] See also Ov. *Tr.* III. 1. 60: *F.* II. 337.

as such, intervene between the preposition and the substantive. Of this the commonest form is:

(1). *p. g. . . .s.*, e.g.

    e speculi...imagine   Ov. *Am.* II. 17. 9.

Ovid affords over thirty instances of this, Tib. I and II two, 'ad digiti...sonum' (I. 2. 32) and 'in dominae...sinu' (I. 5. 26), and Propertius about a dozen, e.g. 'ad lecti...pedes' (III. 6. 14). A complicated case of this occurs at Ov. *F.* v. 228, '*de quorum* per me *vulnere* surgit honor' (= 'quorum de vulnere (= sanguine) honor per me surgit').

    Next in order of frequency is:

(2). *a. p. . . .s.*, e.g.

    imos ante...pedes   Prop. II. 10. 22.

Of this there are two instances in Tibullus,[1] six in Propertius,[2] and about a dozen in Ovid.[3]

    Separation of preposition from an unqualified substantive is less frequent, i.e.

(3). *p. . . .s.*, e.g.[4]

    contra quis feret arma *deos*?   Tib. I. 6. 30.
    trans ego *tellurem*   Ov. *Tr.* IV. 9. 23.

Ovid has no objection to putting the preposition at the end of the hexameter and the 'divorced' substantive in the pentameter, e.g.

    inque | ...patria   *Tr.* IV. 8. 11.
    inter | ...missos (*sc.* equos)   *Tr.* V. 12. 25.

---

[1] I. 9. 44; III. 20. 3.   [2] e.g. II. 9. 25; II. 34. 57; III. 2. 12; III. 7. 10.
[3] *Am.* I. 6. 68; II. 11. 3; III. 6. 63: *H.* IV. 117: *R.A.* 611: *Tr.* IV. 4. 74; IV. 5. 1: *P.* I. 1. 52; I. 2. 150; IV. 10. 2; IV. 13. 1: *F.* V. 348.
[4] See also Prop. II. 9. 18; III. 11. 46: Ov. *F.* V. 351.

(4). *p.* ...*a.* ...*s.*, e.g.

in...humano...loco	Ov. *P.* I. 3. 48.
ad...suos...honores	Ov. *F.* v. 551.[1]

In many, indeed in the majority, of these cases the word
intervening between the preposition and the adjective is connected constructionally with the adjective and forms with it
a single adjectival concept, e.g.

per *mihi cedentes*...aquas	Ov. *H.* XVIII. 76.
ob *huic similem*...culpam	Ov. *P.* I. I. 53.
in *dis invisa*...humo	Ov. *P.* I. 6. 30.
per *sibi consuetas*...vias	Ov. *P.* II. 7. 18.

and in at least one case the adjective is qualified by a qualified
substantive:

ad *molli* declivem *tramite* ripam	Ov. *F.* III. 13.

(5). *s.* ...*p.* ...*a.*, e.g.

poenam fortis *in* ipse *meam*	Ov. *Am.* I. 7. 26.

Ovid has at least half a dozen cases all of which conform to
the type: substantive–verb and/or noun–preposition–*ipse* (*a*)–
possessive pronoun, e.g.

damnis dives ab ipsa suis	*H.* IX. 96.
laetitia solvar ab ipsa mea	*H.* XIII. 116.
indicio prodor ab ipse meo	*A.A.* III. 668.
urbe Coronides vidit ab ipse sua	*Ibis* 406.
discipulo perii solus ab ipse meo	*P.* III. 3. 46.

A much rarer form is

(6). *s.* ...*p.*, e.g.

quae...supra	Prop. II. 6. 38.
quos...penes	Prop. III. 7. 57.

---

[1] See also Ov. *H.* XXI. 180: *P.* I. 8. 1.

Also rare is

(7). *s. p. . . .a.*, e.g.

digitos inter...remissos	Prop. IV. 8. 53.
corpus ad...meum[1]	Ov. *Am.* I. 5. 24.

In the type

(8). *p. . . .a. s.*, the word separating the preposition and the adjective (or participle) seems generally dependent upon, or closely connected with, the adjective (or participle), e.g.

de *prope currenti* flumine	Ov. *R.A.* 618.
a *mihi promisso* corpore	Ov. *H.* XX. 146.
pro *gramen habentibus* herbis	Ov. *Ibis* 401.

These, being equal to *p. a. s.*, are scarcely cases of true tmesis.
A rare type is:

(9). *a. . . .p. . . .s.*,[2] e.g.

Tarpeios...inter...lucos	Prop. IV. 8. 31.

Very rarely the preposition, following and separated from the substantive, immediately precedes the qualifying genitive, giving the type:

(10). *s. . . .p. g.*, e.g.

vada...ad Hebri	Ov. *H.* II. 15.

More elaborate cases are those in which (*a*) the genitive is qualified; (*b*) the substantive is qualified; (*c*) both genitive

---

[1] 'corpus ad usque meum'; *ad usque* and *ab usque* (for *usque ad*, *usque ab*) had been a regular licence since Catullus's time. Cf. 'ad usque limpidum lacum' (Cat. IV. 24).

[2] Ovid has '*talia* succensent *propter* mihi *verba* Tomitae' (*P.* IV. 14. 15).

and substantive are qualified. These usages seem to be restricted to Ovid:

(*a*) (1). *p. ag. s. . . .g.*,[1] e.g.

    inque suae portu. . .salutis   *R.A.* 610.

    in magni templum. . .Martis   *Tr.* II. 295.

(2). *p. ag. . . .s. g.*,[2] e.g.

    de longae. . .flore cicutae   *Am.* I. 12. 9.

    ad Euxini. . .sinistra freti   *P.* II. 2. 2.

(3). *p. ag. . . .g. s.*,[3] e.g.

    ad Pharii. . .piscis opem   *A.A.* III. 270.

    ad vestri. . .favoris opem   *P.* III. 4. 38.

(4). *p. ag. g. . . .s.*, e.g.

    in Getici litoris. . .aquas   *P.* IV. 4. 8.

    inque suae stirpis. . .urbe   *F.* IV. 876.

(5). *p. . . .ag. s. . . .g.*, e.g.

    in mihi promissi parte. . .tori[4]   *H.* VI. 20.

(6). *g. p. ag. . . .s.*, e.g.

    orbis in extremi. . .harenis   *P.* I. 3. 49.

    urbis in Iliacae. . .iuga   *F.* VI. 422.

(7). *ag. s. . . .p. g.*, e.g.

    Aeoliae mare. . .in Helles   *Tr.* I. 10. 15.

    rapidae flammis. . .in Aetnae   *Tr.* V. 2. 75.

(8). *s. g. . . .p. ag.*, e.g.

    tempus lustri. . .in alterius   *P.* IV. 6. 6.

---

[1] See also *P.* III. 3. 19: *F.* II. 464.
[2] See also *Ibis* 443: *P.* II. 10. 1.
[3] *F.* I. 262; 587.
[4] Virtually =*p. ag. s. . . .g.*

In at least one case the place of the adjective qualifying the genitive is taken by a second genitive in apposition:

fratris in Aeneae...funere   *Am.* III. 9. 13.

This is virtually a case of (6).

(*b*) (1). *p. g. a. ...s.*, e.g.
  ad thalami clausas...fores   *A.A.* II. 704.

(2). *g. a. p. ...s.*, e.g.
  carceris obscuras ante...fores   *Ibis* 80.

(3). *a. ...s. p. g.*, e.g.
  dura...terga per amnis   *P.* I. 2. 82.

(*c*) (1). *g. p. ag. a. ...s.*, e.g.
  alitis in rarae miserum...funus   *Am.* II. 6. 9.

(2). *a. ag. ...p. g. s.*, e.g.
  extremam gelidi...in orbis humum   *Tr.* III. 13. 12.

The only other kind of tmesis found in Ovid (it does not seem to occur in the other elegists) is that of such words as *quicumque*, where the *-cumque* is sometimes detached from the first part of the word. Instances are: 'qui...cumque' (Ov. *Am.* II. 14. 40; *Tr.* II. 78); 'quale...cumque' (Ov. *P.* III. 4. 6); 'qualis...cumque' (Ov. *P.* IV. 13. 6).

In one case (*P.* IV. 12. 7) Ovid boasts of abstaining from tmesis. The addressee of the poem is one Tŭtĭcānus, a word which cannot be fitted into any dactylic line. Ovid, however, refuses to end a hexameter with 'Tuti-' and start the penta-meter with 'canus',

nam pudet in geminos ita nomen scindere versus.

(d) HYPERBATON

Hyperbaton is a word that has been used by different writers in different senses. Quintilian[1] calls it a 'verbi transgressio', and regards even the word-order in the sentence 'animadvertisti, iudices, omnem accusatoris orationem *in duas divisam esse partes*' (instead of 'in duas partes divisam esse') as an instance of it. Longinus[2] defines it as the λέξεων ἢ νοήσεων ἐκ τοῦ κατ' ἀκολουθίαν κεκινημένη τάξις; and modern grammarians[3] regard it as no more than a distorted and unnatural order of words.

It is customary, however, when speaking of hyperbaton in the poets, to use the word in a more restricted sense; and it will be used here as meaning the interlocking (anaclasis), in a compound sentence, either of a main sentence and subordinate clause—the more common form—or of the two paratactic parts of such a compound sentence. If a stands for a word in the main sentence and b a word in the clause (or in a paratactic second main sentence), the scheme would be: $aaa\ldots, bbb\ldots, aaa\ldots, bbb\ldots, aaa\ldots$; or $bbb\ldots, aaa\ldots, bbb\ldots, aaa\ldots$: i.e. $n_a n_b n'_a n'_b n''_a$ or $n_b n_a n'_b n'_a$; or, of course, any extended form of this.

On this view of hyperbaton some sentences which have been regarded as hyperbatic should not be regarded as such. For instance when Propertius writes

> tu mea compones et dices 'ossa, Properti,
>   haec tua sunt'   II. 24. 35–6.

we merely have to understand 'ossa' with 'mea'; or again

> nam mea cum recitat, dicit se odisse beatos;
>   carmina tam sancte nulla puella colit   II. 26. 25–6.

'carmina' is to be understood with 'mea'.[4]

---

[1] VIII. 6. 62, 65.   [2] XXII. 1.   [3] Kühner, *op. cit.* II. ii, pp. 618 sqq.
[4] These are cited as examples of hyperbaton by Brandt (on Ov. *Am.* III. 6. 73).

So, too, highly complicated sentences are not necessarily hyperbata, e.g.

> cum multa abstuleris, ut non tamen omnia donet,
> quod nunquam reddas, commodet, ipsa roga
>
> Ov. *Am.* I. 8. 101–2.

(i.e. 'roga (ut) commodet quod nunquam reddas');

> ...nec quemquam Romanum gaudet ab hoste,
> meque minus, vitam cui dabat ipse, capi
>
> Ov. *P.* I. 2. 91–2.

(i.e. 'nec gaudet quemquam R. ab hoste capi, nedum me, cui vitam dabat').

Even the following sentence, contorted as it is, is scarcely to be reckoned as a case of hyperbaton proper:

> non liber hic ullus, non, qui mihi commodet aurem,
> verbaque significent quid mea, norit, adest
>
> Ov. *Tr.* V. 12. 53–4.

(i.e. 'non adest quisquam qui aurem mihi commodet, noritque (= -ve) quid mea verba significent').

Of hyperbaton proper perhaps the commonest type is that involving vocatives, e.g.

> at vos, qua veniet, *tumidi*, subsidite, *montes*
>
> Ov. *Am.* II. 16. 51.

> *parve*, nec invideo, sine me, *liber*, ibis in Urbem
>
> Ov. *Tr.* I. 1. 1.

> at tibi, *rex aevo*, detur, *fortissime nostro*,
> ...sceptra tenere...   Ov. *P.* I. 8. 21–2.

> nunc bene lucetis, *sacrae*, sub Caesare, *flammae*
>
> Ov. *F.* VI. 455.

A second form of paratactic hyperbaton may be seen with *oratio recta*, e.g.

> 'vive' deus 'posito' siquis mihi dicat 'amore'
>
> Ov. *Am.* II. 9. 25.

Cynthia laudavit 'promissa'que 'foedera serva,
    et comitum princeps tu mihi' dixit 'eris'   Ov. *F.* II. 159–60.

Paratactic hyperbaton other than of these two types is rare,
but we find:

Mamurius, morum fabraene exactior artis,
    difficile est ulli dicere, clausit opus   Ov. *F.* III. 383–4.

(i.e. 'Mamurius—(et) difficile est dicere (utrum is fuerit)
exactior morum an fabrae artis—clausit opus');

'hospes', ait 'nosco, Colchide, vela, venit'   Ov. *Tr.* III. 9. 12.

(i.e. 'hospes venit Colchide; vela nosco');

quam tua, rus oculis domini, Campania, gratum
                                        Ov. *P.* IV. 15. 17.

(i.e. 'quam Campania, rus gratum oculis domini, tua (est)').

As instances of syntactic hyperbaton may be cited:[1]

candidior, quod...albet
    et modo siccatam, lacte, reliquit ovem Ov. *Am.* III. 5. 13–14.

(i.e. 'candidior lacte quod albet et modo reliquit...');

si progressa forem, caperer ne, nocte, timebam[2] Ov. *H.* III. 19.

(i.e. 'timebam ne caperer, si progressa forem nocte');

et, mecum, fugias, quae tibi dantur, opes   Ov. *H.* III. 56.

(i.e. 'et fugias opes quae tibi mecum dantur');

Pergama vix...erant repetenda...,
    Hectore, si, vivo quanta fuere, forent   Ov. *H.* VII. 143–4.

---

[1] See Housman in *J. of Phil.* XVIII (1890), pp. 6 sqq.
[2] For this punctuation see Housman in *C.R.* XI (1897), p. 428.

(i.e. 'vix repetenda forent P., si (tanta) forent quanta (erant) Hectore vivo');

illic, qui silices, Thesea, vincat, habes   Ov. *H.* x. 110.

(i.e. 'illic Thesea habes, qui silices vincat');

> . . . nec tu,
> admoneat quod te, pignus, amantis, habes
>
>   Ov. *H.* xv. 103–4.

(i.e. 'nec tu habes pignus quod te amantis admoneat');

> neve putes id me, quod abest, promittere, tempus
>
>   Ov. *H.* xviii. 191.

(i.e. 'neve putes id me promittere quod (=quia) tempus abest');

> tempora qui solis operosa colentibus arva,
>   fallitur, et nautis adspicienda, putat   Ov. *A.A.* i. 399–400.

(i.e. '(is) fallitur qui putat tempora adspicienda (esse) solis (=solum ab) operosa arva colentibus et nautis');

> solus, et, artifices qui facit, usus adest[1]   Ov. *A.A.* ii. 676.

(i.e. 'et usus adest, qui solus facit artifices');

> 'inde, velut nunc est, per quem descenditis' inquit,
>   'arduus, in valles per fora, clivus erat'   Ov. *F.* i. 263–4.

(i.e. '"inde" inquit "arduus clivus erat, per quem descenditis in valles…"');

> ut stat et incertus, qua sit sibi, nescit, eundum   Ov. *F.* v. 3.

(i.e. 'ut stat et incertus nescit qua sibi eundum sit');

> nullaque, quae possit, scriptis tot milibus exstat
> littera Nasonis, sanguinolenta legi   Ov. *Ibis* 3–4.

---

[1] For this punctuation see Housman in *C.R.* xi (1897), p. 428.

(i.e. 'nullaque littera Nasonis (e) tot milibus (ab eo) scriptis (est), quae possit legi sanguinolenta');

> si tamen interea, quid in his ego perditus oris,
> . . . quaeris, agam
>
> Ov. *Tr.* III. 5. 23–4.

(i.e. 'si tamen interea quaeris quid ego (homo) perditus in his oris agam');

> plus isto, duri, si precer, oris ero   Ov. *P.* I. I. 80.

(i.e. 'si precer plus isto, (vir) duri oris ero');

> hoc, ubi vivendum est, satis est, si consequor, arvo
> . . . esse poeta. . .   Ov. *P.* I. 5. 65–6.

(i.e. '(in) hoc arvo, ubi vivendum (mihi) est, satis est si consequor esse poeta');

> quid tibi, si calidae, prosit, laudere, Syenae? Ov. *P.* I. 5. 79.

(i.e. 'quid tibi prosit si laudere calidae[1] Syenae?');

> Parcaque ad extremum, qua, mea, coepit, eat
> Ov. *P.* III. 7. 20.

(i.e. 'Parcaque mea ad extremum eat qua coepit (ire)');

> nec te mirari, si sint vitiosa, decebit,
> carmina. . .   Ov. *P.* IV. 13. 17–18.

(i.e. 'nec decebit te mirari si (mea) carmina vitiosa sint');

> quidve relegatus Naso, requirit, agam   Ov. *P.* IV. 15. 2.

(i.e. 'requiritve quid (ego), Naso relegatus, agam').

It will be observed that all instances of true hyperbaton come from the works of Ovid. The other elegiac writers do not seem to have availed themselves of this licence.

---

[1] Locative.

(e) THREE PECULIARITIES OF TENSE USAGE

(1) *The perfect infinitive used as present infinitive*

The use of the perfect infinitive in sentences where the present infinitive might more naturally have been expected is not peculiar to the elegists, but it is perhaps worth while examining the matter briefly, for it is clearly through this poetic usage that the idiom spread to later prose writers.

The usage goes back to the earliest times when it was restricted to following verbs expressing prohibition or wish.[1] As will be seen from the following list, the elegists stray outside these limits. Verbs, and verbal expressions, after which these perfect infinitives are found, are:[2]

audeo (Tib. II. 1. 9–10).

consilium est (Ov. *A.A.* I. 380).

cupio (Ov. *Am.* II. 2. 10; II. 4. 22; II. 15. 11–12).

cura est (Ov. *A.A.* II. 121–2).

debeo (Ov. *Tr.* IV. 8. 5–12*).

decet (Tib. I. 2. 28: Ov. *Am.* II. 17. 24; *A.A.* III. 145; III. 431–2*).

difficile est (Ov. *A.A.* II. 20).

disco (Ov. *A.A.* III. 455).

est (= 'it is possible', etc.) (Tib. I. 6. 24; *Corp. Tib.* III. 9. 3: Prop. III. 14. 30).

fas est (Ov. *Am.* II. 13. 27).

gaudeo (Ov. *H.* XVI. 202; *P.* IV. 9. 20).

gestio (Tib. II. 1. 71).

[1] Kühner, *op. cit.* II. i, pp. 133 sqq.
[2] An asterisk denotes that both a present and a perfect infinitive are found, e.g. 'monet... | ire nec...timuisse' (Ov. *F.* IV. 131–2).

iuvat (Tib. I. 1. 45–6*; I. 1. 74: Prop. II. 13. 11–12: Ov.
        Am. I. 13. 5; *H.* II. 142; IV. 87–8*; *A.A.* I. 406).

labor est (Ov. *Am.* II. 2. 28; *P.* IV. 10. 82).

laboro (Ov. *H.* XV. 77; XVIII. 95).

licet (Ov. *Tr.* III. 1. 80; V. 12. 45; *F.* VI. 229–30*).

malo (Ov. *F.* VI. 71).

moneo (Ov. *F.* IV. 131–2*).

nescio (Ov. *A.A.* III. 319–20).

noceo (impersonal) (Ov. *F.* III. 191–2*).

onus est (Ov. *M.F.* 22).

opto (Tib. I. 6. 74: Ov. *Am.* III. 2. 30; *A.A.* I. 294).

opus est (Prop. II. 6. 25: Ov. *A.A.* III. 370).

paenitet (Tib. I. 4. 47–8).

paro (Ov. *A.A.* II. 98).

piget (Ov. *M.F.* 47).

possum (Prop. I. 1. 15; I. 17. 1: Ov. *Am.* III. 2. 63–4; *A.A.*
        II. 583–4; III. 333; *F.* II. 322).

probo (Ov. *A.A.* III. 215–16).

prodest (Tib. I. 8. 9–12*).

pudet (Tib. I. 1. 29–30; I. 2. 93–4*: Ov. *H.* IX. 59–60*;
        A.A. III. 769; *F.* III. 282; IV. 367).

pudor (pudori) est (*Corp. Tib.* III. 13. 1–2: Ov. *Am.* III. 14.
    21–2; *A.A.* I. 495–6*; II. 252; *Tr.* I. 1. 50; *F.* I. 205–6).

queo (Tib. I. 9. 63–4*; *Corp. Tib.* III. 11. 16).

satis est (Tib. I. 10. 61–2*).

timeo (Ov. *H.* XV. 172).

turpe est (Ov. *Am.* I. 10. 41–2*; *A.A.* I. 733–4; II. 215–16;
        P. II. 6. 21–2*).

tutius est (Ov. *Am.* II. 11. 31–2; *H.* III. 117–20).

utile est (Ov. *R.A.* 626).

virtus est (Ov. *H.* XVII. 98).

volo (Tib. I. 4. 56; I. 6. 64; *Corp. Tib.* III. 12. 6; III. 12. 18:
 Prop. II. 19. 32; IV. 3. 70: Ov. *Am.* I. 4. 38; II. 4. 26;
  II. 17. 30; II. 19. 56; *H.* III. 110; *F.* IV. 86).
voluptas est (Ov. *M.F.* 31).
vota sunt (Ov. *A.A.* I. 579).

Perfect infinitives, often in conjunction with present infinitives,
are occasionally found after present tenses of verbs of pre-
tending, saying (being said), seeming, thinking, and seeing;
and it is not always easy to say whether the perfect infinitive
in these cases has a real perfect sense or whether it furnishes
another instance of the use of the perfect infinitive as equal
to the present infinitive. Some such cases are:

simulat...condoluisse caput   Tib. I. 6. 36.

('that she has a headache' or 'that a headache has come on');

dicatur...bibisse... | ...vel...emeruisse   Tib. I. 9. 59–60.

('that she is in the habit of drinking' or 'that in her lifetime
she has drunk');

saepe...onerare...
  saepe...videor supposuisse   Ov. *H.* XV. 127–8.
hoc stulti non valuisse putent   Ov. *A.A.* I. 730.
non...ullum gaudere...
  auguror, at multos indoluisse   Ov. *Tr.* II. 569–70.
aspicis...pallere...?
  aspicis...intremuisse...?   Ov. *Tr.* III. 1. 55–6.

After such introductory verbs in the *perfect* we find instances
of the same thing. Here it is probably a case of tense attrac-
tion, e.g.

vidistis...percurrere...
  fulminaque...desiluisse   Prop. II. 16. 49–50.

| quae voluit legisse, volet rescribere lectis | Ov. *A.A.* I. 481. |
| visus (est) adesse... \| et dixisse | Ov. *F.* II. 504–5. |

Over and above the metrical conveniences of this use and the doubtless welcome touch of archaism, we may perhaps see in it a more or less conscious use by the Latin elegists of the Latin perfect infinitive as if it were a Greek aorist infinitive.

(2) *The pluperfect used as imperfect or perfect*

This, again, is not an exclusively poetical usage. It seems to have sprung from colloquial idiom,[1] to have been used freely by the elegists, and so to have passed into ordinary (later) prose.[2] Any pluperfect might be thus used, though *fueram* standing for *fui* or *eram* is probably the commonest.[3]

Tibullus seems to have fought shy of this idiom, of which he affords but one definite[4] instance, 'haec fuerant olim' (II. 5. 79). There are in Propertius[5] some two dozen instances:

(a) Pluperfect for imperfect

cum...adfueram	I. 10. 1–2.
non sum ego qui fueram	I. 12. 11.
non sic...Calypso | ...fleverat...; | ... | ...sederat	I. 15. 9–12.
turba...fuerat nec...tanta	II. 6. 3–4.
primos mugiverat annos	II. 28. 17.
Callisto...erraverat	II. 28. 23.
nudi fuerant	II. 29. 7.
circum steterant armenta	II. 31. 7.
terra parum fuerat	III. 7. 31.

---

[1] Kühner, *op. cit.* II. i, p. 141.

[2] See K. F. Smith, *Tibullus: the Elegies*, on II. 5. 79.

[3] It is likely that *fueram* derives from the combination of *fui* and *eram*: Lindsay, *op. cit.* p. 509; H. Blase, *Geschichte des Plusquamperfekts im Lateinischen* (Giessen, 1894), p. 47.

[4] Perhaps also 'fueras...laesurus' (I. 9. 1) and 'auxerat' (II. 1. 58).

[5] See Butler and Barber on I. 8. 36.

nec fuerat...poena	III. 13. 38.
exsequiae fuerant	IV. 5. 71.
luxerat igne casa	IV. 9. 28.

(*b*) Pluperfect for perfect (preterite)

quas Elis opes...pararat	I. 8. 36.
Thessalus...venerat	I. 19. 10.
quae miser...error... | Herculis...fleverat	I. 20. 15–16.
quas pastor viderat	II. 2. 13.
turba... | venerat	II. 29. 3–4.
dulcis...fuerat...rixa	III. 8. 1.
haec di condiderant	III. 11. 65.
palluerant...labra (*nisi leg.* palluerunt)	IV. 8. 54.
riserat	IV. 8. 82.

In several cases it is likely that '-ĕrunt' should be read for the MSS. '-erant'. So Butler and Barber in II. 8. 10; III. 24. 20; IV. 7. 15. They would also read 'fuerunt' at 'quae fuerant ...inimica' (I. 11. 29; 'which have (always) been inimical'). If 'fuerant' be retained here, it furnishes the only instance in Propertius where a pluperfect stands for a true perfect.[1]

Ovid seems to have used this colloquialism less often (comparatively speaking) than Propertius. It is true that he often has constructions like '*dixerat*, illa deum promisso ludit inani' (*F.* III. 685), or '*dixerat*, *et* plenam non firmis viribus urnam \| sustulit' (*ib.* 39–40), but in these cases 'dixerat' should probably be regarded as a true pluperfect, and the whole sentence as a mere parataxis for the normal (prose) syntactical form 'cum dixisset...ludit' or 'sustulit'. Besides (the usual) 'dixerat' Ovid writes, e.g.

Iuppiter adnuerat. nutu tremefactus uterque	
est polus	*F.* II. 489–90.
adnuerant Rutuli; Mezentius induit arma	*F.* IV. 891.

[1] On this subject see Housman in *Proc. of Class. Ass.* 1921, pp. 82 sqq.

As instances of his idiomatic use of the pluperfect may be cited:

(*a*) Pluperfect for imperfect

non satis id fuerat	*H*. v. 69.
quid minus...fuerat sperare	*A.A*. III. 429.
quot fuerant Argo lumina	*A.A*. III. 618.
non sum ego quod fueram[1]	*Tr*. III. 11. 25.
qua steterant Artes	*P*. I. I. 12.
qui fueram globus	*F*. I. 111.
lilia deciderant	*F*. v. 317.[2]

(*b*) Pluperfect for perfect (preterite)

haec mihi narraras	*H*. VII. 85.
dictus eram...venisse... | ...induit	*A.A*. III. 245–6.
munera quae dederas habeat	*R.A*. 671.
sus dederat poenas	*F*. I. 353.
venerat...Silenus	*F*. I. 399.
tu dederas transilienda Remo	*F*. II. 134.[3]

(3) *The 'double' pluperfect with passive verbs*

By this is meant a pluperfect passive made up not of the combination of the past participle and the imperfect of the verb *sum*, but of the past participle and the *pluperfect* of *sum*: e.g. 'amatus fueram'. These verbs are like those dealt with under (2) in *form*, inasmuch as, with them too, *fueram* stands for *eram*, but they are always pluperfect in *meaning*.

[1] Cf. Prop. I. 12. 11.

[2] Other instances may be seen at *Am*. I. 13. 34; III. 8. 3: *H*. I. 115; XII. 69: *A.A*. II. 475: *Tr*. IV. 2. 28; v. 12. 30: *P*. II. 3. 61; III. 2. 53; III. 3. 37; IV. 9. 119: *F*. I. 635; III. 224; IV. 429; v. 133; v. 610; VI. 254.

[3] Other instances at *A.A*. II. 172; II. 478: *R.A*. I: *Tr*. II. 337: *P*. I. 3. 47: *F*. I. 364; II. 737; III. 213; III. 232; III. 706; IV. 897; v. 537; VI. 625; VI. 722.

The usage is not exclusively poetical.[1] As instances may be cited:

fueram...patefacta	Prop. I. 16. 1.
quam fuerant (nota)	Prop. II. 13. 38.
Andromede...fuerat devota	Prop. II. 28. 21.
amborum fuerat confusa voluptas	Ov. *H.* XV. 49.
quam laesus fuerat partem	Ov. *R.A.* 111.
fuerat genitus	Ov. *P.* IV. 14. 33.
quae fuerat virgo credita (esse)	Ov. *F.* II. 176.
quae fuerat...amata	Ov. *F.* II. 182.
fuerat promissa potentia	Ov. *F.* VI. 359.

[1] Kühner, *op. cit.* II. i, p. 164.

APPENDIX A

Demonstrative Pronouns

It is a curious fact that whereas all the elegists use the demonstrative pronouns *hic*, *ille*, and *iste*, freely in all, or almost all, their cases,[1] they evince a marked aversion to *is*, or at least to most of its cases.[2] The only forms of this pronoun used with any frequency are *is*, *id*, and *eă* (feminine singular and neuter plural); and even these are used sparingly by the two earlier poets. Tib. I and II has *is* at I. 2. 39–40; I. 10. 66; II. 3. 33; Propertius has *is* at II. 32. 1 and perhaps II. 32. 52 (other MSS. read 'hic'), *id* at I. 20. 2, *eă* at II. 9. 36 ('sive ea causa gravis, sive ea causa levis'). Ovid on the other hand has about forty instances each of all three.

Of the other cases:

eum: Tib. (Lygd.) III. 6. 12: Prop. II. 29. 8 (uniquely at the end of the pentameter); III. 20. 1: Ov. *F.* IV. 551; VI. 584; VI. 755.

eam: Prop. III. 6. 9 (if the reading is right): Ov. *H.* VII. 15; *P.* III. 6. 25; *F.* I. 721; II. 254; VI. 434 (accepted by Frazer, but almost certainly wrongly).

eius: Tib. I. 6. 25: Prop. IV. 2. 35; IV. 6. 67 (both these at the end of the hexameter): Ov. *Tr.* III. 4. 27 (end of hexameter); *P.* IV. 15. 6.

ei (dative) does not occur in elegiacs.[3]

---

[1] *istorum* and *istarum* are not found, and *illarum* perhaps only at Prop. I. 13. 9; *harum* perhaps only at Prop. II. 34. 51.

[2] The figures for Virgil are: *eă* (forty), *id* (twenty), *is* (sixteen), *eum* (ten), *eo* (four), *eā* (two), *eam* (one).

[3] There is a case in Ovid's *Halieuticon*, 34.

eo: Ov. *H.* XII. 69; XX. 29; XX. 240; *P.* I. 2. 101 (if genuine); *F.* IV. 146.

eā: Prop. II. 1. 46: Ov. *H.* XV. 182; *R.A.* 301; *Tr.* II. 429.

The plural forms are even rarer. Neither genitives, datives, nor ablatives are found at all, and of the accusatives perhaps only *eos* at Prop. II. 21. 7. At *F.* v. 150 Ovid ends a pentameter with 'eă est'.

APPENDIX B

Note on the *Consolatio*

The *Consolatio ad Liviam*, which has sometimes been attributed to Ovid, is clearly non-Ovidian, from a metrical standpoint, in at least three respects: (1) it contains an unusually large percentage (10·55%)[1] of fourth-foot weak caesuras in the hexameters; (2) it shows an excessive number of elisions of long vowels and diphthongs; (3) it has three non-caesural hexameters (ll. 35, 379, 449). Over and above this, elisions are found at places where Ovid seldom if ever uses them. Such are:

(*a*) elision at half-way point of the pentameter:

collaque et osque oculos(que) ‖ illius ore premam   34.

(*b*) elision of long open vowel at second diaeresis of hexameter:

nec nocuisse ull(i) | et fortunam habuisse nocendi   47.

(*c*) elision of long open vowel at second diaeresis of pentameter:

ultima: sit fat(i) | haec ‖ summa querela tui   76.

(*d*) elision of *-am* at third diaeresis of pentameter:

lumina et excipias hanc anim(am) | ore pio   158.

---

[1] Normally 6%; see p. 10.

118

BIBLIOGRAPHY

OF BOOKS, DISSERTATIONS, AND ARTICLES

(Those works that I have been unable to consult are marked with an asterisk.)

ATKINSON, R. 'On the trisyllabic endings of the pentameter in Propertius.' *Hermathena* I (1874), pp. 276–85.

AXELSON, B. *Unpoëtische Wörter.* Lund, 1945.

BAEDAE *Opera historica*, ed. Plummer. Oxford, 1896.

BEDNARA, E. *De sermone dactylicorum latinorum quaestiones.* Vratislava Diss., 1905.

BIRT, T. *Ad historiam hexametri latini symbola.* Bonn Diss., 1876.

BLASE, H. *Geschichte des Plusquamperfekts im Lateinischen.* Giessen, 1894.

BRANDT, P. *P. Ovidi Nasonis Amorum libri tres.* Leipzig, 1911.

BRANDT, P. *P. Ovidi Nasonis De arte amatoria.* Leipzig, 1902.

BRAUM, O. *De monosyllabis ante caesuras hexametri latini collocatis.* Marburg Diss., 1906.

BUTLER, H. E. & BARBER, E. A. *The Elegies of Propertius.* Oxford, 1933.

*CAVALLIN, C. *De caesuris quarti et quinti trochaeorum hexametri apud latinos poetas coniunctis.* Lund, 1896.

CORNU, *see* LIEGER.

EHWALD, R. *P. Ovidius Naso* (tom. I). Leipzig, 1903.

EHWALD, R. & LEVY, F. W. *P. Ovidius Naso* (tom. III). Leipzig, 1922–4.

*EICHNER, E. *Bemerkungen über den metrischen und rythmischen Bau des Catull, Tibull, Properz, und Ovid.* Gnesen, 1875.

EICHNER, E. *De poetarum latinorum . . . distichis quaestionum metricarum particulae duae.* Soaru Diss., 1866.

*ENGBERS, B. H. *De metricis inter Tibulli Propertique libros differentiis.* Rostock Diss., 1873.

ENK, P. J. *Sexti Propertii elegiarum liber I.* Leiden, 1946.

*ESCHENBURG, B. *Metriche Untersuchungen über die Echtheit der Heroides des Ovids.* Lübeck, 1874.

FRAZER, Sir J. G. *The Fasti of Ovid* (5 vols.). London, 1929.

HARKNESS, A. G. 'The word-group accent in Latin hexameters.' *Classical Philology*, III (1908), pp. 39 sqq.

HARTENBERGER, R. *De 'o' finali apud poetas latinos.* Bonn Diss., 1911.

HILBERG, I. *Die Gesetze der Wortstellung im Pentameter des Ovid.* Leipzig, 1894.

HÖRSCHELMANN, W. 'Ueber die Elision bei Tibull und Lygdamus.' *Philologus, N.F.* X (1897), pp. 355 sqq.

HOSIUS, C. *Propertii elegiae* [3]. Leipzig, 1932.

HOUSMAN, A. E. Articles in *Classical Review*, XI (1897), pp. 102 sqq.; 200 sqq.; 238 sqq., etc.; XIII (1899), pp. 172 sqq.; XXXIII (1919), pp. 56 sqq.: *Classical Quarterly*, X (1916), pp. 130 sqq.; XXI (1927), pp. 1 sqq.: *Journal of Philology*, XVIII (1889), pp. 1 sqq.; XXI (1893), pp. 160 sqq.: *Proceedings of the Classical Association*, 1921, pp. 67 sqq.

HULTGREN, E. F. *Statistische Untersuchungen des Distichons.* Leipzig, 1872.

HUMPHREY, M. W. 'Accent in Latin dactylic hexameter.' *Transactions of the American Philological Association*, IX (1878), pp. 39–58.

KÜHNER(-HOLZWEISSIG). *Ausführliche Grammatik der lateinischen Sprache* (vol. I). Hanover, 1912.

KÜHNER(-STEGMAN). *Ausführliche Grammatik der lateinischen Sprache* (vol. II). Hanover, 1912–14.

LEUMANN, *see* STOLZ & SCHMALZ.

LIEGER, P. *J. Cornus Beiträge zur lateinischen Metrik.* Vienna, 1927.

LINDSAY, W. M. *The Latin Language.* Oxford, 1894.

MERKEL, R. *P. Ovidius Naso*[2] (vol. III). Leipzig, 1904.

MEYER, W. *Zur Geschichte des griechischen und lateinischen Hexameters.* Munich, 1885.

MIRGEL, H. *De synaloephis et caesuris in versu hexametri latini.* Gottingen Diss., 1910.

MÜLLER, L. *De re metrica poetarum latinorum*[2]. St Petersburg & Leipzig, 1895.

NORDEN, E. *P. Vergilius Maro, Aeneis Buch VI*[3]. Leipzig, 1926.

OWEN, S. G. *P. Ovidi Nasonis Tristium libri V.* Oxford, 1889.

OWEN, S. G. *P. Ovidi Nasonis Tristium liber secundus.* Oxford, 1924.

PALMER, A. *P. Ovidi Nasonis Heroides.* Oxford, 1898.

PHILLIMORE, J. S. *Sexti Properti carmina*[2]. Oxford, 1907.

PLATT, A. 'On the Latin pentameter.' *Classical Review*, XXXIV (1920), p. 168.

POSTGATE, J. P. *Tibulli aliorumque carminum libri tres.* Oxford, 1904.

RADFORD, R. S. 'The juvenile works of Ovid.' *Transactions of the American Philological Association*, LI (1920), pp. 146–71.

RAMSAY, W. *Manual of Latin Prosody*[7]. London, no date.

SCHOENER, C. *Ueber ein Gesetz der Wortstellung im pentameter des Ovids*. Erlangen, 1896.

SIEDOW, A. *De elisionis aphaeresis hiatus usu in hexametro latino ab Ennii usque ad Ovidii tempora*. Greifsw. Diss., 1911.

SMITH, K. F. *Tibullus: the Elegies*. New York, 1913.

STOLZ, F. & SCHMALZ, J. H. *Lateinische Grammatik* (fifth ed. by M. Leumann & J. B. Hofmann). Munich, 1928.

VOLLMER, F. *Gercke-Norden, Einleitung in die Altertumswissenschaft* (vol. I, sect. viii). Leipzig, 1923.

WHITEHEAD, P. B. 'A new method of investigating the caesura in the Latin hexameter and pentameter.' *American Journal of Philology*, LI (1930), pp. 358–71.